WINNING HIGH SCHOOL BASKETBALL

• **Jay McCreary**

Edited by Bob Barnet, Sports Editor, Muncie *Star*

PRENTICE-HALL, INC.

Englewood Cliffs, N. J.   1956

Library of Congress Catalog Card Number 56-11007

Printed in the United States of America

96084

To the many fine boys

whom I have been privileged to coach

Foreword

Jay McCreary, as an eminently successful coach, is well qualified to write a book on high school basketball. Having been a competitive, aggressive player and an excellent assistant and head coach, he understands the problems of high school boys and has a thorough knowledge of the techniques of basketball. Jay played his high school basketball on the state champion Frankfort, Indiana, team. At Indiana University he played three years of varsity basketball for me and was a member of our 1940 NCAA championship team. His Vincennes High School teams were outstanding. And, as my freshman coach at Indiana University, he further proved his ability to work with and understand the problems of ballplayers. His knowledge of the fundamentals and systems, and his ability to teach them, have produced teams with exceptional basketball "know-how."

Jay coached successfully at DePauw University before going to Central High School, Muncie, Indiana. At DePauw his teams were outstanding in their league for aggressiveness, competitiveness, and basketball knowledge. During his coaching career at Central High School, he

and his teams have been familiar figures at the Indiana
State Basketball Tournament, having won the tournament
in 1952 and 1954 being runners-up in the final four.

An enthusiastic student of the game, Jay is continually
learning and improving styles of play to suit his material.
His players respect him both as a coach and as a man.
Every coach feels a great deal of pride and satisfaction when
one of his former players is successful. I am sure that Jay
McCreary's book, *Winning High School Basketball,* will
be most helpful to all coaches.

BRANCH McCRACKEN
Basketball Coach,
Indiana University

LEGEND FOR DIAGRAMS

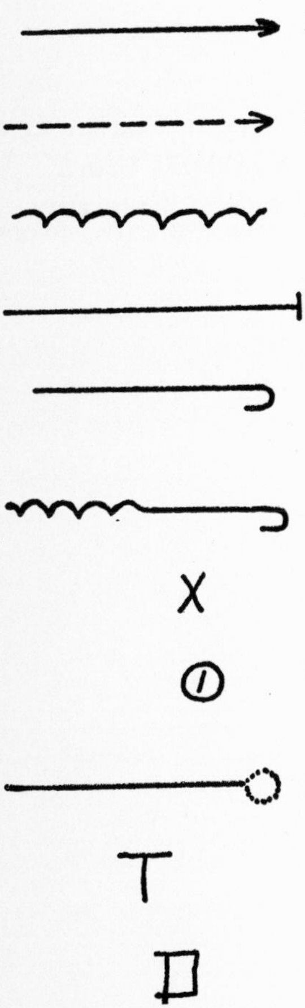

———————⟶ *PATH OF PLAYER*

– – – – – –⟶ *PASS*

‿‿‿‿‿‿‿ *DRIBBLE*

——————⊣ *BLOCK*

—————⊃ *REAR TURN*

‿‿‿———⊃ *DRIBBLE AND REAR TURN*

X   *OFFENSE*

⊘   *DEFENSE*

————————○ *MOVEMENT OF DEFENSE*

T   *TRAILER*

⊓   *DEFENSE VALVE ON FAST BREAK*

MANY OF THE IDEAS AND PRACTICES EXPRESSED IN THIS BOOK I have worked out through twenty-seven years of association with the game of basketball as a player and coach. In many instances these ideas have been gathered at coaching clinics, from textbooks on basketball, and from the numerous articles in the *Athletic Journal* and other magazines. To these many coaches—for their many valued ideas and suggestions—my sincere thanks.

JAY MCCREARY

Contents

● The high school basketball coach

D R. JAMES A. NAISMITH, ALTHOUGH HE APPEARS TO HAVE been equipped with all the enthusiasm of a good YMCA man, wouldn't have believed it.

During the 1954–55 school year a total of 19,592 high schools were members of athletic associations affiliated with the National Federation of State High School Athletic Associations. Of that number, 18,775 were represented by teams striving earnestly to win at the sport that the Springfield, Massachusetts, physical education director gave to the world in 1891.

1

Basketball is the crew-cut king of prep sports. No other athletic pastime comes close to threatening its reign. National Federation figures, compiled by Secretary H. V. Porter, reveal that 95.8 per cent of all member high schools sent out basketball teams in 1954–55. A distant second in the race for interscholastic sports supremacy was baseball, with 60.5 per cent of the schools represented. Track teams wore the colors of 55.2 per cent, with eleven-man football played by 47.1 per cent and six- or eight-man football by 10.5 per cent.

All states except California, Delaware, and New York determined state prep basketball champions in 1955. In California and New York contending teams were reduced to sectional champions. More than one million high school boys played interscholastic basketball during the school year, and the number playing some type of basketball was something over two million.

Oddly enough, high school basketball isn't growing much these days. It can't, having practically reached the saturation point. Nearly all schools that do not now send forth prep basketball squads are not represented only because equipment is not available. The spirit is willing, if the budget is weak.

No high school sport—few athletic endeavors of any kind—have more impact on the community. The high school basketball team is public property. It belongs to the entire community because it is made up of the kid in the next block multiplied by five.

In Indiana, admittedly a basketball hotspot, basketball tourney time spawns a sort of mass hysteria that astounds and often frightens outsiders not aware that all Hoosiers return to normal the day following the championship game—or nearly normal! The 1955 Indiana state prep tournament was witnessed by a total of 1,483,211 happy ticket-holders, some of whom, of course, stood in line all night to purchase precious pasteboards.

High school basketball being the healthy young giant that it is, the high school coach, for better or worse, is an important citizen, a big man in his community. There are nights when it would be necessary only to open the polls to make him mayor, or even governor. There are other nights when he forsakes the familiar sidewalks of his home community for the alleys thereof.

His job is of tremendous importance because the young men who come under his control have reached an age at which characters are moulded, an age at which the line between worthwhile young manhood and juvenile delinquency is a thin line, and dim.

No schoolteacher is more imitated than the athletic coach. And the basketball coach holds a particularly strong position because he represents the sport most American high school boys want to play. He has few unwilling pupils.

The oldest joke of the coaching profession insists that character is taught when the stars have been graduated. But the greater number of high school basketball coaches *do* teach character, every day, in every practice session, in every game. Their opportunities are limitless and, with few exceptions, they are men who believe earnestly that a good boy is a more worthwhile product than a good basketball player, a decent citizen more valuable than a championship.

The high school basketball coach, like his opposite number in other sports, generally is a valuable member of his community, a good teacher, and a good father. Aware that it is the rule, rather than the exception, for a boy to pattern his life after that of his coach, he strives to lead a life that will withstand public scrutiny. He is a public figure, bound by the restrictions that exist for all public figures. He is also a man proud of his job—and should be.

But it is just as easy to teach character with a winning team as with an habitual second-placer, and this book is offered with the hope that it will help produce, if not victories, at least near misses. The professional life of many a coach has been saved by a moral victory. The near miss is not to be spurned.

Readers will note that great stress is placed on hard work on the part of coach and players. The writer has concluded that there is no substitute. Basketball victories are not fashioned by dropping pennies in a wishing well. It is necessary to drop basketballs into baskets, frequently and with precision. If this can be done with style and aplomb, so much the better; but it must be done somehow.

Hard work, material, and luck—these are the essentials for the winning basketball team. The coach who has no material may nurse to his bosom the oft-forlorn hope that he will get some next year. But the coach who doesn't believe in hard work, for himself as well as for his athletes, is in the wrong business. So, perhaps, is the coach who is unlucky. The ball so often drops the wrong way.

Because he deals with a nation's most precious raw material—its youth—it is impossible to overestimate the importance of the schoolteacher. With the exception of the parent and the clergyman, no individual has more impact on the future of his community, his state, and his country than the instructor who, in addition to reading, writing, and arithmetic, teaches American young men and women to become happy, tolerant, worthwhile citizens.

From the moment a child enters kindergarten the teacher is in contact with him through a far greater share of his waking hours than is the parent. The schoolteacher

accepts a task that is exacting and difficult. He shoulders
a responsibility that often is frightening.

The high school coach faces an assignment even more
complex since he, in addition to classroom activity, must
teach his athletes to meet squarely the problems en-
countered in competition. He must help them build
strong bodies as well as strong minds. His job is perhaps
more important than that of the ordinary schoolroom
teacher, because athletic competition often produces
obstacles similar to those the athlete will meet in the
day-by-day battle to live and rear his family. He must learn
tolerance and self-restraint. He must learn to get along
with his fellow-man. He must learn to fight back.

A coach worthy of his profession is aware that his community and his school want him to turn out good citizens
first, good athletes second. Because young men of high
school age generally admire and imitate their coach, it is
obvious that the coach must be a decent, moral man
capable of setting a proper example. If he is a "wrong
guy" his players are very likely to be "wrong guys" also,
and throughout their lives.

Coaching should be a pleasant occupation. The coach
should enjoy his work. Athletes should enjoy the sport in
which they participate. When basketball or any other
sport ceases to be fun for a boy, he should find some other
outlet for his energy. And coaching *is* pleasant, and there
is fun for everyone. But there is a stern, underlying truth
to which all coaches must face up: that theirs is a God-
given opportunity to steer young men in the right direction. Taskmaster and big brother, disciplinarian and
father confessor, teacher and seeker of knowledge, the
coach is all these things, and more.

Must the coach be a crusader? Not at all. He needs only
to be a gentleman whose day-to-day conduct is in keeping

with the traditions of sportsmanship and clean living. He needs only to be the kind of coach he would want for his own son.

THE COACH'S EDUCATION

The man who would be a high school basketball coach should bear in mind that he is first a teacher, then a coach. He must learn to teach, to impart to others the knowledge that is his. It is plain that the greatest basketball player of all time would fail as a coach if he were unable to pass along his knowledge.

Although some good coaches are nonplayers, it may be seen readily that actual participation in basketball as a high school or college varsityman gives the prospective coach an invaluable background. He hasn't had to learn everything from books. He *knows*, because he has been a player. If he has been a varsity player he is also likely to be humble enough to know that a man's learning never stops and that, if he learned one thing as a player, it was that he didn't know enough.

Player or nonplayer, the prospective coach should enroll at the best possible college. If he wishes to teach in a particular state he should attend a college in that state, because he will become known, if he is a player, to the schoolmen and newsmen with whom he will be in contact as a coach.

It is not possible for every young man who wants to be a coach and who wants to play college basketball to earn a place on the varsity team of a great university. Unless he is good enough to play on a top team, it is often better for him to enroll at a smaller school, since he can learn far more basketball by playing in a lower classification than by being cut from the squad at a big university.

Excellent basketball courses in nearly all the nation's colleges send the young man into the coaching world equipped with everything but luck and experience. The former he may or may not have in his pocket—the latter must be written into the books on a day-by-day, month-by-month, year-by-year basis.

The coach must continue to be a seeker of knowledge long after he has completed his college education. Since he is a teacher, he must strive always to be a better teacher, to learn new teaching methods, to keep pace with the times. As a coach he must be humble enough to study the work of more experienced coaches and flexible enough to borrow from the methods of men who already have met and solved the problems that trouble the young coach. The sincere coach attends all coaching clinics in his area and is an avid reader of books and magazine articles on his particular sport.

In short, the wise coach studies his chosen profession as a doctor or lawyer studies his profession. He strives always to be a better coach. Likely to be a steady loser is the complacent fellow whose methods are antiquated and who does nothing about it. The good coach "grows" as the years pass.

Coaching is hard, monotonous, grinding work. It is often discouraging. The faint-hearted belong in some other business. Lazy coaches don't win consistently, nor do coaches who lack the patience to teach the same thing over and over and over again, until that happy day when a high school boy has learned his lesson.

At Muncie Central, when we lose or win in a lackluster performance, we have a standing comment for our basketball patrons and members of the press: "We start all over Monday!"

That's coaching: starting all over again after you thought

your team was ready to roll and keep on rolling. It's a
hard way for a man to make a living. It's also wonderful!

THE NEW JOB

As is the case in professional athletics, it is often the
policy of school officials to replace coaches whose teams
fail to win consistently. It has been shown earlier that high
school basketball is big business. Teams that do not win
do not draw well. Since basketball often carries the financial load for the entire sports program of a high school,
it is necessary that basketball be financially successful.

These things being true, the high school coach must
accept as a part of his life occasional shifts to other communities. Not many schools insist that a coach win all
his games, but not many like him to lose them all. Usually
there is nothing personal about a shift in coaches. It is just
an occupational hazard.

Often the coach moves for the opposite reason, because
he has been so successful that he is offered a job at a bigger
school, one that moves in a higher bracket of competition.

It is well to remember that no coach finds things
exactly to his liking in a new position. He must be able
to adapt himself to existing conditions, rather than charg-
ing full-tilt into a new arena, determined to "run things"
in his own way.

THE NEW COACH AND THE SCHOOL
ADMINISTRATION

Because he is to be a part of an unfamiliar organization,
the new coach must study that organization carefully to
make certain he fits into his proper place. Before accepting

the job, he should have a thorough understanding of his duties as coach and faculty member. It is wise for him to learn whether he is expected to perform such extra-curricular duties as club sponsor and chaperone for school functions.

In nearly all cases the coach is responsible directly to the principal, who in turn is the liaison man with the school superintendent, school board, trustee, and state athletic association.

It is well to learn whether the school operates its athletics from a written list of policies and to request a copy of such a list if one exists. If there are no written policies, the coach is well-advised to ask that all traditional school policies and customs be explained to him fully.

The coach needs to know whether the arrangement of schedules is his responsibility or that of the principal or athletic director. He is likely to find that the schedule for his first season already has been completed. If the schedule is not complete, it is his place to meet with the person responsible for the schedule to make sure that it is filled as soon as possible.

It is well for him to request an inventory of basketball equipment on hand and learn whether athletic budgets have been drawn up, and by whom. The coach needs to know who buys equipment and from whom it is to be bought. At this point in his conference with the principal or trustee the coach may find an opportunity to point out that, if he is to purchase equipment, he should be permitted to seek quality rather than be tightly bound by price restrictions and the necessity of purchasing from local merchants, even when they cannot furnish the type of equipment desired.

All teams travel and the coach must have a clear understanding of travel arrangements. The writer personally believes that a team travels best by chartered bus whenever possible, since it is more comfortable and players, coaches, and others are fully covered by insurance. It is possible to travel at less expense by individual automobiles if the school desires, although that mode of travel often is not satisfactory. When the entire team rides in a single large vehicle, like a bus, the coach may discuss team problems and plan with all his players for the approaching game. Bus travel also affords an opportunity for team comradeship that is lacking when the squad is divided.

The athletic budget is the determining factor in the purchase of meals for athletes. The writer believes that meals should be the best possible and has learned that it is best to arrange for meals in advance, especially for those following a game and for a team that is traveling. When we are convinced that no satisfactory restaurant is on our travel route, we carry our meals, usually sandwiches and milk. This procedure is far better than a half-dozen cases of illness because of unwise eating on the road.

Care of injuries is another subject that must be covered by the coach in one of his early conferences with the school administration. Is the coach privileged to send a player directly to a physician or a hospital, or must he first contact the principal or another school official?

Obviously the length of practice sessions is the business of the coach, but starting time for practices should be cleared with the principal. The coach must know in advance when his gym will not be available for practice because of other activities in the building.

The new man plainly needs to know who hires his assistants. Ordinarily the present assistant, if he wishes to remain, will fill the position adequately and will be of great value to the new coach because of his knowledge of the players who will make up the new man's first team.

Should the coach feel that a policy needs changing, he is within his rights to talk over the matter with his principal or trustee. In this way he will be able to present his own viewpoint and obtain that of the school administration. He should be reasonable and considerate of other coaches.

But no principal, superintendent, or trustee likes to be told that his program is antiquated and should be junked immediately. Some school officials are eager to profit by the fresh ideas of the new coach. But a great many others feel that the old way is good enough. The coach must remember that he is the coach and normally does not make athletic policies, but only carries them out.

THE COACH AND THE FACULTY

Since high school athletes must remain eligible scholastically if they are to remain in uniform, the coach is extremely vulnerable to faculty action. That being the case, it is necessary for the coach and other faculty members to operate in an atmosphere of mutual respect and understanding. Cordial relations with faculty members are merely common sense, and the coach does well to remember always that he himself is a faculty member, not an outsider wrangling with strangers. He must be able to understand the problems of the teacher and usually it is possible for the coach, by means of friendly conferences, to help the teacher understand the problems that are a part of the coach's job.

The problem of player grades often is a difficult one because there are faculty members in every school who make no secret of their distaste for athletics in any form. But these teachers usually react favorably if the coach makes it plain to them that he wants no preferential treatment for his athletes. Players must be made to understand that their coach does not intend to help them "get by" and that he will not go with hat in hand to faculty members or seek to intimidate them. Athletes who know that their coach expects them to measure up to the classroom standards that exist for nonathletes, with no help from him, are likely to knuckle down to the job that must be accomplished if they are to remain eligible. No intelligent coach asks a "free ride" for an athlete. Rather than from the faculty, the best help in preserving a player's eligibility often comes from the parents.

The coach will find that other faculty members will note with approval his willingness to be a part of school activities not connected with coaching. He must bear in mind that his sport is only a part of the general program. A narrow-minded attitude makes friends only among that segment of the school population that is characterized as "basketball crazy." A good many folks can take basketball or leave it, and the coach does well to keep that fact in mind.

THE COACH AND THE COMMUNITY

The high school basketball coach is an important man in his town. Nearly all residents of a community are interested in its schools. This is a normal situation, since sons, daughters, grandchildren, and neighbors have been, are at present, or will be school pupils. Since high school athletic contests usually are viewed by large audiences, many citizens become acquainted with their schools through high school athletics.

Guiding spirit of the team, the coach is respected and admired so long as he merits that respect and admiration. The coach finds it's easy to sell himself and his program because members of the community want to like him. He should affiliate with church, fraternal, and civic organizations and take an active part in community life. Whether he likes it or not, he is a public figure and must accept the inconveniences that often accompany public acceptance. If he doesn't like to hear the telephone ring, if he objects to becoming "community property"—often at the expense of his homelife—then he should not turn to coaching, because that is part of the game.

The coach should, as often as possible, accept speaking engagements. People are interested in him and in his athletes. They want to hear about them. If he does become a public speaker, he should confine his orations to the subject he knows best—basketball. His listeners want to hear about basketball or he wouldn't have been invited to speak. And he should keep it brief!

THE COACH AND THE PRESS

There are a number of outside factors with which the high school coach must deal. One of the most important is the press. When a high school begins selling tickets for its games it offers merchandise and asks a price. People who sell merchandise must advertise. Few high schools could afford to pay for the thousands of lines of publicity that are written about their teams in the nation's newspapers or broadcast over radio and television. This is free publicity and it behooves schoolmen, including coaches, to remember that they are being given something that a newspaper is not required to give. True, the newspaper's patrons demand news of their schoolboy athletes, but every newspaperman knows that reports of high school sports could be presented in far less space than they are now given, should publishers decide to be less generous.

It is of vital importance for the high school coach and the men covering his team for newspapers and other outlets to work together in mutual respect. An unfriendly press makes a hard job harder, and only a foolish coach deliberately makes enemies among the men at the typewriters and microphones.

The coach should strive always to be impartial with news releases, especially if his community has more than one newspaper or radio station. News that breaks in time for the morning paper should be offered that paper. The coach should never hold out news for the benefit of a favored individual, but should be honest and fair with everyone who covers his team.

The press is a great moulder of public sentiment, and the coach can often use it to get his ideas across to the community. Newspaper stories are invaluable in building team and community spirit. Players read the papers and, if they have confidence in the writer, they believe what they read. A capable writer, if he knows the right things to say, often is of great help in bringing a team to fighting pitch for an important game or tournament. Newsmen generally know what they are doing and generally want to help the coach and his team. But most of all, they are duty-bound to print and broadcast the news. Good or bad, they must print it, and it is well for the coach to know and understand the aims and ideals and responsibilities of the men whose profession is so closely allied with his own.

THE COACH AND HIS PLAYERS

Good mental attitude is as important as a good shooting percentage. No team is consistently successful unless its players are convinced that they cannot perform as glory-grabbing individuals but as members of a tightly knit unit. The coach must be a part of that unit. The relationship between a coach and his players is vitally important. Players must respect and trust the coach, and he can earn this respect only by being honest with the young men with whom he is to be in close contact through a long season.

A good many coaches—far too many—undermine the confidence of their players before the season even opens by falling victim to one of the oldest temptations in the coaching profession. They weep loudly, to all who will listen, that all the good players departed last Graduation Day. They insist that the current array will be lucky to win even one game. Unwise? Of course such conduct is unwise, since it infers that the leftover personnel is of poor quality and that little is expected of it. The "Gloomy Gus" in the coaching racket usually is a man looking for an alibi.

The good coach is honest and reasonable in discussing team prospects with patrons, players, and members of the press. Just as he should never tell his team that it is the world's best, he should never tell a group of high school athletes—no matter how sorry their performance—that they are the world's worst. He deals with his players as young men, not children, outlining the task they face and their prospects for success. He reminds them of the rewards for work well done.

High school athletes usually can be reached by man-to-man treatment. The coach must be completely honest with his players in all things and certainly can never be less than honest about the quality of their opposition. He levels with them always, and on all subjects.

It is impossible to bring a team to real fighting pitch for every game. This "priming" is best done rarely, if at all. Boys often will "come up" without help if they know the situation and want keenly to win. The wise coach avoids continual harping about things badly done and mixes constructive criticism with commendation if the latter is in order.

At Muncie Central we have had many slogans on our locker room walls. If the writer were required to choose just one, it would be:

WHO PASSED THE BALL WHEN YOU SCORED?

Every team has players who are more efficient than their mates. While recognizing that fact, the coach should attempt to play down the "star" angle by dwelling on the value of self-sacrifice and team spirit. He should make it plain that every position is open and that a reserve or second-team player who is good enough to move up will get that position.

Strict training rules are not always essential. But the high school coach should expect his players to use common sense in eating, sleeping, dating, and exercising. When it is obvious that a player isn't in proper physical condition, he should be given a long rest—on the bench. Players who fail to get and stay in good playing condition soon eliminate themselves, especially in a "Go, go, go!" system. While discussing health problems it might be well for the coach to remind his players that they, not the school, benefit most from their participation in athletics. Parents often are helpful in solving problems pertaining to conditioning.

Team discipline can never be relaxed, although the good coach is always on good terms with his athletes. He does not, however, forget that he is the coach and they the players. He can never meet them on purely common ground—he is the boss.

The wise coach is never too busy to talk with a father

or mother. He answers honestly their requests for information about the progress of their son.

The writer also believes in being honest with his players about their ability to play college basketball. If the player isn't a bigtime college prospect, the coach should tell him so. In advising players about college, the coach should keep in mind the requirements for the type of education the player seeks. If he wants to be an engineer he should go to an engineering school. If there are no interfering factors, the high school coach is fully within his rights in recommending to the college-type player the coach's own alma mater.

Nearly any coach, watching his squad in practice, is able to detect signs of overconfidence. Our coaches move quickly when such signs are observed. We change an overconfident player's attitude quickly, or an empty uniform hangs in the equipment room until a more interested youngster is moved up from the reserve team.

The place of the coach after a game is with his team, especially if his team has been defeated. In his own disappointment, the coach must never forget to give commendation when that is due. He seeks to restore lost morale. Defeat has a bitter taste for a high school athlete who has done his best. He needs his coach then, and the coach needs patience and understanding and the determination to make these lads winners.

The game is played to win, because victory, with honor, should be the goal of every athletic team. There should be no patience with the boy who does not hate defeat or who offers an alibi for defeat. No one should be satisfied with defeat. Basketball players should be poor losers—although silent losers—if they are to be winners when they play the game of life. The world already has too many docile losers.

two

• The high school feeder system

I N THAT OTHER WORLD TO WHICH GOOD COACHES GO
when they leave this referee-infested vale of toil and
trouble, it is possible that each newcomer is handed a
magic wand that, when waved gently to and fro, produces
ready-made basketball players whose shots never stray,
whose defense is above reproach, and whose nimble legs
never tire. This may be the case in Heaven, but it isn't like
this down here!

Bigtime college coaches get polished material. High
school coaches take what they get and do their best to make
something of it. The logical answer—the only answer—is
a well-planned, smoothly functioning feeder system, in
which basketball players begin learning their lessons as
early as their grade school years.

The test of a feeder system is in the won-lost record of the high school team toward which the system channels its material. Our Muncie teams have been consistent winners and we feel therefore that we can call our feeder system a good one, although it is never forgotten in our planning and is improved to the best of our ability as the years pass.

Muncie Central has its high school athletes during three school years—sophomore, junior, and senior. The freshman year is spent in junior high school. Players are far from polished when they come to us, although it has been possible in a few instances to call on sophomores as varsity starters. These cases are rare indeed and the boys involved were of the "one-in-a-thousand" type who attain top skill and physical maturity early in life.

Our feeder system graduates have a solid basketball background. Our feeder system coaches are aware that their players will need much detailed work, much "smoothing out," after we get them. But the players come to us with a general idea as to our pattern of play.

The Muncie Central feeder system gives us a wide selection of player talent. We are fortunate in that our system includes a group of junior high schools with all the elementary schools channeling players through the large junior high schools.

All coaches with experience know that material comes in cycles. In a small school the good cycle turns up perhaps every four or five years. Our feeder system, admittedly a large operation, is designed to shorten the cycle. But the cycle is always there, no matter how large the school.

Even in a high school of nearly 2,000, bulwarked by a carefully constructed feeder system, we do not get great players every year, or even especially good ones. Our size, however, enables our feeder program to produce two or three passably good players nearly every year. This could be done only with a good feeder system. Fine players don't just happen along.

It is probable that All-Americans are born, not made. But the solid, serviceable players who will shoulder the greater part of the burden for a high school coach *are* made, and are not a gift from a generous Providence. And making good players of high school boys is just plain hard work.

The most important single factor in the successful feeder system is the calibre of coaches in the junior high schools. Although instruction often starts when boys are only grade school pupils, the junior high school teachers are the men who have most to do with getting varsity players ready for the big step to the "big" team. Each coach sends his boys into 12 to 18 games each season, and by the time a boy reaches his sophomore year he will have played in 45 to 50 games. Thus, in addition to his hour-after-hour work in fundamental drills, the player is given actual participation and the thrill of belonging to a team that actually plays a schedule.

It should be pointed out here that in Muncie all our junior high school coaches, while they like to win, are perfectly willing to sacrifice won-lost records to work with players who we have decided are varsity prospects, even though their work as junior high school players is not so efficient as that of others. Our coaches never lose sight of the fact that the ultimate goal is a strong *high school* team. They are dedicated to the task of producing Bearcat teams that are capable of winning, rather than junior high school teams that go undefeated. This is done with no desire to kill the desire to win among our younger players. Boys and coaches strive to win every game, but the lads who do the playing are those who we think possess the potential to be good players as senior high school athletes.

The same system is followed in organized baseball, in

which boys who are considered major league prospects are given far more opportunity in minor league competition than players designated by wise old baseball men as "service ballplayers," whose careers will be spent solely in the lower levels of the game.

It may be that we have raced ahead of our story in an effort to make plain the great importance of the job done by our junior high school coaches. Almost as vital is the work of men whose "varsitymen" are far younger. We have in Muncie fourteen elementary schools and one parochial school whose students ultimately arrive at Muncie Central. Other students in the community attend Burris School, a laboratory school for Ball State Teachers College.

Burris, which has its students from the first grade through the senior year, maintains its feeder system in its own school and has done remarkably well through the years. Although smaller than many township schools, Burris has on two occasions qualified for the four-team state finals tournament and once played in the championship game.

In each school of the Central system we have a fifth grade coach and a sixth grade coach. The schools are divided in a north-south league and play a round-robin schedule, with division winners meeting for the city championship. A handsome trophy is awarded to the winning school. In addition, each elementary school conducts an intramural basketball program that goes as low as the third and fourth grades. One school conducts a basketball league for girls.

Great enthusiasm exists in all the schools. Elementary school basketball in Muncie is fun, and should be fun. But we try to give the youngsters an understanding of the rules and the more simple fundamentals. We want them to do things correctly right from the start.

Our elementary school coaches use a standardized course of instruction designed to acquaint youngsters with the proper methods of doing things without turning the game into drudgery. We want them gradually to do the right things instinctively, and those not familiar with our system often are surprised at what they call the "natural talent" of players reporting to junior or senior high school coaches. Much of that talent, of course, isn't "natural" at all, but the result of careful planning and proper instruction. The boys learn by doing and still derive great pleasure from their hard-fought games.

Elementary drills are divided into offensive, defensive, and team categories. Offensive drills include dribbling, with team relay races involving dribbling around obstacles, stopping, turning, and passing; passing, in which various types of passes are demonstrated by the coach; and shooting, in which the players take part in long-and-short and other shooting games, practice layup shots from both sides of the basket, and drill consistently on the one-hand jump shot from the foul circle area. They hit those nine-foot-high baskets, too!

During work on defense players take part in group drills in which the entire squad follows the coach in proper defensive footwork. One-on-one drills stress proper defensive techniques, and players are sent through position drills for under-basket work and rebound drills in which the defensive men receive rebounds, turn, and look for an open man.

Team drills include work at one end of the floor in game situations, team offensive and defensive formations, fast-break drills, rebounding, ball-advancing before the defense is set, in-bounds drills, and extensive scrimmage. They get the whole package, those lads, and they love it!

Practice periods generally are one and one-half hours in length and are held twice each week. It is customary to play one game weekly, except at tournament time, when two games usually are played each week and practice is reduced to one session.

Approximately 90 per cent of the practice time is devoted to individual drills early in the season. But as the season progresses more and more time is given team drills, with the result that at tournament time the ratio is 90 per cent of the practice time in team drills, 10 per cent in individual work.

Equipment is obtained from a number of sources. Usually the school budget provides some money for balls and other supplies. Junior high school teams often pass along worn equipment, including uniforms. Equipment often may be purchased from the school general fund, which is raised by ice cream socials, bake sales, and other school and parent–teacher events.

Though no prizes or trophies are awarded individual players in elementary basketball, all are given recognition at special school programs near the end of the year.

In looking for high school varsity prospects, the elementary coach usually judges his players by the following formula:

A. Coordination.
    1. Does he succeed in football and track as well as in basketball?
B. Interest.
    1. Does he want to be outstanding?
C. Does he accept instruction, or is he a know-it-all?
D. Social adjustment.
    1. Does he get along well with classmates and teachers?
E. Academic ability.
    1. Does he use all his potential in the classroom?
F. Home background.
    1. Do his parents want him to succeed in school work and athletics, or are they indifferent?
G. Natural ability.
H. Rate of improvement.

It will be noted that drills and procedures set up for

our elementary athletes are similar to those given high school varsitymen. Although it may appear that elementary youngsters are given too great a load, this actually is not the case, since instruction is given informally by coaches who never lose sight of the fact that basketball is a game to be played and enjoyed. The popularity of the program among elementary students is demonstrated by the fact that in every school in our system there are more candidates than the coaches can use, and squad cutting is necessary, even at that level.

THE JUNIOR HIGH SCHOOL FEEDER SYSTEM

The Muncie Central feeder system is in operation in four junior high schools, each of which has teams representing the seventh, eighth, and ninth grades. Each of the three teams has a coach and each plays a complete schedule.

Seventh grade basketball. In screening candidates for seventh grade teams, coaches attend elementary school games and see each session of the city elementary tournament. They are in close contact with elementary coaches throughout the year. Likely candidates are invited to try out in early November, and others are added as they are discovered in physical education classes.

In screening, coaches look for players who have the ability to remember and carry out assignments. Natural ability, coordination, and scholastic record are factors considered. The squad is cut to eighteen players and the team plays twelve to fourteen games each season. Games are played on an after-school basis, usually starting at 3:30 P.M. Offensive and defensive drills are those used by senior high school players. Practice hours are 5:30 to 7:30 P.M. each weekday except on days of games. School records and home backgrounds are checked periodically.

Eighth grade basketball. During the first week of the season an open call is issued, but the squad is soon reduced to 25 players. During the first week of practice emphasis is on individual drills in such fundamentals as shooting, meeting the ball, passing, and footwork. Defensive and offensive drills are conducted, with players taught the techniques used by senior high school players. Training routines and academic responsibilities are explained.

During the second week fundamental drills are continued and offensive drills expanded. Players are taught the use of screens and blocks. Scrimmage is held on a two-on-two and three-on-three basis and offensive pattern options are explained. Scrimmage is then conducted over the entire floor and players are reminded of the value of team play.

During the remainder of the season practice routines include the usual fundamental drills. Weaknesses observed in practice and in games are corrected. Charts are kept for general player analysis and as a check on specialized skills, like shooting. The eighth grade team plays fifteen to eighteen games and takes part in one tournament.

Ninth grade basketball. Ninth grade coaches meet with seventh and eighth grade coaches at the start of the season to examine charts of individual players. Each player is thoroughly discussed.

The first call is limited to members of the eighth grade team of the previous year. Other ninth-graders who may have developed during the summer are given an opportunity to try out three days later. The squad is cut to fifteen after one week of practice. Practice sessions are held from 3:30 to 6 P.M. each weekday and on Saturday mornings during November and December.

Practice routines include work in shooting, dribbling, passing, footwork, defense, rebounding, offense patterns, defense patterns, and scrimmage. All fundamentals are taught according to the desires of the senior high school coach, who meets with junior high school coaches often to outline proper technique and obtain information on the progress of individual players. The patterns used are basically the same as those used by the high school team, although junior high school coaches are free to experiment within certain bounds. The ninth grade team plays sixteen to eighteen games each year, in addition to one tournament.

Each team receives the sum of $150 annually from the senior high school, to be used for the purchase of equipment. Uniforms of a solid color are purchased one year, white uniforms the next. Uniforms two years old are passed along to the eighth grade team, and from that team they are passed to the seventh grade team. Warmup uniforms are given the ninth grade team by the senior high school team. Seventh and eighth grade team members wear T shirt warmups, purchased by the junior high schools. Basketballs also are purchased by the junior high schools. Shoes, supporters, socks, and practice uniforms are furnished by players, soap and towels by the junior high schools.

It should be noted that at all three junior high school team levels great stress is placed on fundamentals. Offensive and defensive patterns of all three are basically those of the senior high school team.

Excellent cooperation is given senior high school coaches by those in the junior high schools. All junior high school teams travel by schoolbus. Meals are furnished only during tournaments. Milk is given players after each home game.

The one-hand jump shot is taught and encouraged in all three grades, although other shots are taught and their uses explained. Greatest stress is on the one-hand jump shot.

All junior high school coaches are available for scouting at the request of the senior high school coach.

It should be made clear that our system does not function solely for basketball, or even for athletics. It has produced football, track, baseball, and wrestling teams that have been consistent winners.

Basketball and football teams have won state championships and Central has produced many individual state champions in track and wrestling. We even have a feeder system in music, and our Muncie Central band, directed by Don Parlette, won the national high school band championship during the Cherry Blossom festival in Washington, D.C., in 1954. Good high school musicians, like good high school athletes, don't just happen.

Cooperation among elementary, junior high school, and senior high school coaches is of vital importance in the successful feeder system. There is no jealousy among Muncie Central coaches, since our common goal is success for our Bearcat teams—in every sport! A high school athlete should be permitted to take part in any sport in which he is interested, so long as he is able to carry the normal scholastic load. No effort should be made, as is often done in college, to force a boy to specialize in a single sport. A high school boy rarely has had time to find out which sport is his best. He should be given the opportunity to learn whether his principal skill is in basketball or in football, track, or baseball. No coach should tell an athlete he will be penalized if he tries out for another sport. Such an attitude is dangerous because it fosters jealousy among coaches and quickly tears down school spirit. Why shouldn't a good football end play basketball? He has the hands for it. Why shouldn't a fast basketball guard run the dashes for the track coach if he is blessed with the necessary straightaway speed?

NAME BIRTH DATE

HT. WT. I.Q.

POSITION PLAYED

GRADE SCHOOL COACH

SPORTS OTHER THAN BASKETBALL

PARENT OR GUARDIAN HT. WT.

RESIDENCE PHONE

OCCUPATION RELIGION

REMARKS OF 6TH GRADE COACH

JR. HIGH_____

7th Grade	8th Grade	9th Grade
I. Q. START OF SEASON Ht. Wt. END OF SEASON Ht. Wt.	I. Q. START OF SEASON Ht. Wt. END OF SEASON Ht. Wt.	I. Q. START OF SEASON Ht. WT. END OF SEASON Ht. Wt.
Weak Points	Weak Points	Weak Points
Strong Points	Strong Points	Strong Points
Remarks	Remarks	Remarks

Cumulative card used in evaluating junior high school players.

All our coaches offer their services in scouting. The writer often has served as a football scout and some of his own scouting has been done by track, baseball, and football men.

Often during the basketball season we take our junior high school basketball coaches to out-of-town games. On the way home we sit together on the team bus and talk over the performances of boys who were turned out by the junior high school coaches and who now are with the senior team. Junior high school coaches offer invaluable advice on the personalities and playing problems of particular boys because they often know the boys better than the senior high school coach, who may have met them only a few months earlier.

In Indiana the high school basketball season starts officially November 1. We start work October 1. During the first week in October we conduct a conference for senior and junior high school coaches. We discuss players who have moved up to Central from the junior high schools. Each junior high school coach presents a brochure he has prepared on each player he has sent to Central. (A sample is shown in Figure 1.) Each player is rated and each coach offers his opinion about players of other teams in the system. In this way the senior high school coaches are given a complete picture of each sophomore prospect. It is only good business practice to watch personally as many junior high school games as possible during the season.

Junior high school schedules should include at least twelve games, most of these against teams of other schools. Boys want to play. They want to play different opponents and they learn by playing if their efforts are properly supervised.

The feeder system in smaller schools must be built on a

more restricted basis, but no school is too small for an intelligent system of player selection and instruction. An intramural program is often a valuable aid in discovering players of more than ordinary natural ability. If coaching help is not available it is possible that someone in the community—a former player, perhaps—will lend assistance if asked. Every school has sports followers who want to help. How better can an alumnus or ordinary sports patron help than by offering a hand in the all-important task of finding and polishing players for future years?

A good feeder system is not developed overnight. Two or three years may be necessary to make it work, but the coach who establishes such a system is a wise one. The good feeder system pays off in victories.

• Picking the players —the preseason program

THERE ARE SCHOOLS IN WHICH THE COACH, STARTING AT a new job or beginning a fresh season, approaches his gymnasium fully aware that he will take what he finds and make do with it. There are schools in which it is difficult to recruit enough able-bodied players to man varsity and reserve squads. This situation, of course, presents to the coach one of the problems that makes his job

31

interesting. But most coaches, were they asked to ballot on the subject, would vote for more players and a less interesting job.

To the coach in a position to choose from a sizable squad of candidates—and happily he is in the majority—the portion of this chapter devoted to player selection is directed. Preseason practice suggestions are for everybody.

The new coach must bear in mind that basketball followers in the community in which he is beginning operations are divided into two schools of thought. Representatives of one want victories, and in a hurry. Others are willing to give a new coach a fair trial and the time to install his system and make it work. The wise coach does not lose sight of the fact that, although he has been hired on the basis of past performance, he still is expected to perform creditably in his new assignment. Like his players, he cannot "get by" for long on last year's press clippings. These things make the selection of player personnel one of the most important tasks facing every coach.

It is well to have a thorough understanding with prospective team members before practice begins. Already curious about the new coach, players have a right to know what he wants of them. At once the coach should make it plain to his players that he asks them to make no sacrifices that he himself would not make. Since he will require them to work hard, the coach must make it plain that he himself is ready to work hard to make the season a successful one.

The basketball coach is fortunate in that his season does not open until several weeks after school has begun in September. He may use this interval to good advantage in learning to know prospective varsitymen and in making unexpected appearances wherever groups of high school boys are playing impromptu games. He may find good players there—players who wouldn't turn out for the varsity team without an invitation because they didn't believe they were good enough for varsity basketball.

The coach, especially the new coach, will find that many persons are ready and willing to offer opinions as to the capabilities of players. Although he should be friendly and courteous in accepting this advice, even when it comes from complete strangers and persons who obviously don't know a hook shot from a jump ball, the coach must bear in mind that it is he who will pass final judgment on each player who wears the uniform of his school. Good sources of information as to player capabilities are elementary and junior high school coaches, faculty members, and newspapermen who have followed the team in the past. The good coach has an open mind on this subject and accepts all possible information to assist in cataloguing his players.

Even when he has put together a rather complete file on a player, the coach reaches the point at which he himself will be called upon to make a decision regarding that player. The knack of picking the right player for a particular job is the thing that separates the good coach from the fair coach. No coach should jump to conclusions regarding a player. The decision as to his individual fitness is best answered when the player is seen under fire.

In selecting his varsitymen, it is well for the coach to look for players who can "take coaching." Occasionally, during a winning streak, a player will begin to show unmistakable signs that he knows all there is to know about basketball. This player and the coach go into conference immediately and the player is reminded that, since the coach himself is learning new things every day, then there must be a few things that the player still doesn't know. This type of logic usually deflates the young man and he is a better and wiser player thereafter.

THE PRESEASON PROGRAM

In many states the high school athletic association establishes the date on which basketball practice may open. But most state high school athletic associations have no objection to preseason conditioning campaigns conducted by the players themselves. Many prospective varsitymen play volleyball, skip rope, run, and play handball.

The first call for candidates should be directed to all boys in the school. In nearly all the larger high schools the first call for basketball overlaps the football and cross-country seasons. Arrangements can be made for these boys to report later without penalty. At Muncie Central we strictly enforce a gentleman's agreement among coaches that football and crosscountry athletes will be required to stick with their squads until their seasons have ended and they are released to basketball by their coaches. Such an arrangement might not be necessary in some areas. In Indiana, where basketball is king, it definitely is necessary. Without it a good many football and crosscountry athletes would drop their sports the day basketball practice opened. Obviously such a condition would be unfair to other coaches and to the nonbasketball players who would be left to fight their way through late-season games and meets with squads at less than full strength.

We do not furnish equipment during early basketball practice, but issue complete uniforms after the final squad cut.

When practice opens we outline the fundamentals that must be mastered by each player and do our best to convince him of the value of practice in fundamentals. We stress footwork, ball handling, pivoting, passing, shooting, dribbling, cutting, faking, defensive stance—all the things a good player must know instinctively. It is obvious that such a program, when a large squad of candidates is present, overloads the coaching staff. But it is often possible to pass along some of this preliminary work to veteran players, who usually are eager to help.

Drills are conducted on an individual basis when work begins. Each fundamental skill is demonstrated by the coach, after which the squad is divided into groups for practice in these skills. Groups are kept as small as possible so that personal attention can be given boys needing special help. When groups are small, all players are active and never find it necessary to stand around while waiting a turn.

Two-man drills follow individual work, and here an element of competition can be injected. It should be noted that in all cases we drill on styles and formations that are used in our system. There is no point in giving players skills they will never use.

The first week is devoted to fundamental drilling and players are required to perform each action in a certain way. Because of our efficient feeder system, we have a good idea as to the capabilities of nearly every player who comes to us. But we always watch for the "sleeper"—the boy who may have developed quickly or who may have been overlooked in our elementary and junior high school screening. Some young men mature suprisingly during the summer between their ninth and tenth years in school.

REDUCING THE SQUAD

The humane coach would like to keep every boy who seeks to earn a place on his squad, but obviously he cannot do this. Players should be given every possible chance to make good and released only after the coach is convinced that in that particular year they cannot make the grade. At Muncie Central only the obvious misfits are eliminated during the first week. The serious cutting job begins during the second week, when we continue to work on fundamentals but also begin scrimmaging.

We divide the boys according to their position preferences, and from these forward, center, and guard groups teams are selected for scrimmage games. Players are shifted often to positions other than those they desire, since we believe that a player should be able to operate either at forward or guard. We never worry about the score in scrimmage games but ask ourselves certain questions about each player. Does he move easily? Does he willingly carry his share of the defense load, or is he strictly a shooter? How does he react to changing situations? Does he appear awkward? (Look out for this one, Coach. Remember, it's still early in the season. He may not shoot well either, because he may not have practiced shooting for a year.) Does he play well with others? Will he be a team man or a lone wolf? What is his school classification? (It is obvious that the sophomore should be given preference over the senior, all things being equal.)

After the first cut we check the scholastic standing of each boy remaining with the squad. His conduct in school and around town is given careful inspection. One bad boy can ruin a basketball team. We want no rowdies, no matter how well they shoot. While we are not too concerned about his intelligence quotient, we want him to be sufficiently intelligent to remain eligible. A great many boys of only average intelligence have a certain genius with a basketball.

Players who appear capable of fitting into our system are retained and others, as we decide their individual cases, are called aside and told courteously that they are not yet ready to play with our varsity and reserve teams. If the boy has questions, they are answered promptly. If he feels that he has not done his best up to that time and is capable of better effort, we permit him to try again. If, after a second inspection, we still believe that the boy is not up to the task, we tell him so. Still, if he is an underclassman, we encourage him to become a member of a church league, YMCA, or industrial league team in order to gain playing experience. And we make it plain that he is welcome to try again next year. Being dropped from the squad is a bitter pill for most young athletes, but they respect the coach who is honest with them and leave the gym feeling that they have been given a fair chance.

After the final cut we return to fundamentals. After football and crosscountry athletes have reported, the process of cutting is repeated, and after a second squad reduction we go back to those ever-present fundamentals and slowly work into our defensive and offensive patterns. Scrimmage activity is stepped up, since this type of practice often serves as a counterbalance for the endless drilling in fundamentals and other such work. We usually carry twenty to twenty-five players for our "A" and "B" squads.

Coaches are not always in agreement as to the qualifications for a sound basketball player. Generally, the qualities sought are: speed, natural ability, good mental attitude, good height, willingness to cooperate, agility, and the ability to be a leader.

No effort has been made to list those valued characteristics in order of importance. The writer isn't even certain as to which is the most important. He knows only that he seeks them endlessly among young players. Often a few are present, and now and then comes that great moment in the life of a coach when he finds a player who has them all. Or has he?

four

● Fundamentals

A TIME-TESTED RECIPE FOR RABBIT STEW OPENS WITH this earnest morsel of advice: "First catch a rabbit." Skill in fundamentals is the rabbit that must be apprehended by the successful basketball team. It isn't enough to call fundamentals an important part of the game—they *are* the game!

The player who appears to float without effort into position, who shoots accurately, who seldom is caught in a tight spot, who scoops up a loose ball and turns someone's misplay into two points for his own team—he is the player who has been well grounded in fundamentals. He wasn't born that way, although admittedly some athletes appear to have been given more than their share of natural ability.

Coaches who slight fundamental drills will see their teams beaten by simple errors that should not have been committed. It is the task of every coach to sell his players on the value of efficiency in fundamentals, to make them willing to drill and drill again until correct fundamental procedures are so well learned that they never will be forgotten.

The player who does not grasp the value of skill in fundamentals not only hurts his team, but himself as a player. He will always be a substitute, while the regulars —and the stars—will be the players who are willing to stick with a phase of their basketball education that admittedly is monotonous.

During an important game one of our Muncie Central teams trailed by three points with only one and one-half minutes to play. We substituted a player who promptly hit four successive field baskets, two from each side of the court, enabling us to pull out a victory. He wasn't lucky. He knew how to shoot!

Players who come to us from our feeder system, although they normally are well grounded in fundamentals, often must be required to discard certain bad habits in fundamentals. They may have discovered that they can execute a required movement in a manner that seems easier to them. They are informed politely but firmly that there is no shortcut to perfection and that perfection is our goal.

It is necessary for the coach to demonstrate correct procedures, then insist that his players follow his example in every detail. The good coach is quick to detect a bad habit and equally quick to correct it. High school boys often learn things suddenly, perhaps after the coach has despaired of putting across his message. Patience is the keynote here, as in so many phases of coaching.

Every coach, old-timer or beginner, must build his

offense and defense on a foundation of good fundamentals. Complicated play formations often fascinate the new coach, but if he faces up to reality he will confess that no offensive pattern will function unless his players are skilled in passing, faking, dribbling, shooting, and the other everyday skills. Fundamental efficiency is the horse that comes before the cart.

In his work *Psychology and the School,* Cameron speaks of the value of good player habits. "Provided an activity is one that will be performed frequently," he writes, "it is advantageous to make it habitual, for it will then be performed with greater ease, greater speed, and greater precision." Certainly few will find fault with that theory!

This is the procedure followed at Muncie Central to demonstrate fundamentals at the beginning of the season. Perhaps the drill concerns the parallel stop. Players are called to the center of the floor and asked to sit. The writer and his assistant each have one basketball. No conversation among players is permitted, since we want the full attention of every athlete. The parallel stance is demonstrated, after which we ask for questions. We explain the why's of the stance and list its uses. Following the demonstration, players are divided into small groups and players execute the maneuver as coaches visit the groups in turn, making corrections and offering encouragement if it is warranted.

The player is required to execute the drill in the same way each time, since he is forming a habit and we want it to be a good habit. We stay with it until we are satisfied. Players often run through a drill as many as a hundred times, but when one of our players finds it necessary to employ the parallel stop during a game he doesn't have to think about the mechanics of the movement. He just stops! The writer once knew a coach who often stood behind a chair and spent half a practice watching players sprint up to the chair, then stop. It is likely that none of those players ever will forget the proper method of performing that particular maneuver.

HITTING THE TARGET

Like the cold-eyed sheriff of the Old West, a basketball team retains the respect of its adversaries and of the citizenry in general only if it knows how to shoot and is perfectly willing to start pulling the trigger. The one-hand jump shot is the weapon that lays them low in modern basketball. With this fearsome piece of ordnance, which has come into general use only in recent years, little ones bring down big ones. It is the great equalizer.

The sudden popularity of the one-hand toss is one of the more curious aspects of a game that has had its share of drastic changes. Coaches who a dozen years ago would have screamed like wounded panthers had one of their young athletes been guilty of such recklessness now devote much of their practice time to wistful search for a one-hand gunner who never misses. The one-hand jump shot, launched from any point on the court and at any time, is the number one weapon in present-day basketball. It is here to stay.

By the time a boy becomes a high school sophomore his shooting habits, for better or worse, are rather firmly fixed. Personally, the writer does not care how a player shoots, so long as he is able to hit the basket. A field basket that is the result of an unorthodox shot still counts two points. Such shooters are welcome in our gym, so long as the ball goes where we want it to go.

This does not mean that we do not make changes in

the shooting form of individual players. A boy may hit 30 per cent of his shots, but if careful study convinces us that he is capable of hitting 35 per cent we make the necessary alterations in his style. We do not go to extremes but seek to correct such minor errors as dropping the ball to the butt of the hand before shooting, shifting the fingers prior to release, falling away while shooting, taking the eyes from the basket, and using poor finger position. Perhaps his wrist action is wrong, or he shoots off balance and fails to follow through. Perhaps he has a habit of shooting from out of range.

When adjustments are made we station the player close to the basket, perhaps five feet away, and ask him to shoot. Gradually he is moved back until he learns his maximum effective shooting range. We encourage him to shoot each shot in the same manner. We require him to set his sights on the center of the hoop, then use the arch that suits him best. A correctly placed shot drops just over the front edge of the rim.

Use of the bankboard for an angle shot is a subject on which coaches do not agree. The writer feels that it is best to disregard the board entirely except for layups, hook shots, and shots taken at the end of a dribble.

In shooting, body balance must be good. The shooter must be relaxed. The fingertips control the ball and the ball is never palmed. The follow-through is an important part of every shot. The wise player takes good shots and avoids "prayer" shots he *hopes* will go into the basket.

The layup shot. The layup is essentially a short-range shot in which the ball is "laid up" against the bankboard. It usually is taken by a player who has escaped his defender or has received a pass while close to the goal. He may have cut past the pivot man, received a lob pass from a teammate, or dribbled into position for the layup.

In executing the layup from the right side the player uses his right hand. The takeoff foot is the left and spring comes from the left leg. Added momentum is gained by lifting the right leg The ball is firmly grasped by the fingers and thumbs of both hands and carried above the head. The right hand is at the two o'clock position and the left at the eight o'clock position. The back is straight, head up, and eyes are focused on the basket. Just before the ball is released the left hand is removed and the ball rests on the right hand as on a tripod. The last point of contact is the fingertips. The right arm is fully extended. The left arm serves to protect the shooting arm from the defender. The ball is laid softly against the bankboard within the painted rectangle above and behind the goal.

At the conclusion of the shot the palm of the right hand is facing the bankboard. The player, after the shot is released, returns to effective playing area as quickly as possible. If the layup shot is properly executed the ball requires little or no spin, or english. The shooter making a layup shot high jumps. He never broad jumps.

On a drive-in layup from directly in front of the basket all fundamentals are the same regarding takeoff foot, ball-handling, and position of arms and hands. We have a standing rule that a player who cannot "dunk" the ball—get above the goal and drop the ball through—must use the board on a straight drive-in shot. Many coaches will disagree with this theory, but we have discovered, through careful chart work, that our percentage is noticeably higher when we use the board instead of attempting to lay the ball over the front edge of the ring.

Use of the bankboard on the frontal layup is easy to teach. The player, on his last step, swings either to the right or left of the basket and uses the same motion as in the side layup shot. He does not throw his arm in a wide arc. This is sometimes used by a player in an effort to avoid his guard, but if the body position, between the defensive man and the ball, is proper, there is no need for moving the arm in an arc.

We do not permit our players to turn the back of the hand toward the basket while making a layup shot. Since the ball must pass over the ends of the fingers, this sacrifices ball control. We have discovered also that many shots hit the bottom of the rim and bound out when this kind of layup is used.

The one-hand push or jump shot. Here is a shot that may be used by every member of the team. It is the most popular shot of our time. It may be used from any point on the court within effective range and the effective range depends largely on the individual shooter. However, we do not shoot at ranges longer than twenty feet unless we need a basket desperately and time is running out. The shot may be taken at the end of the dribble, from a set position, or when a pass is received. We fake before shooting in order to force the defender to yield shooting room.

The mechanics of the jump shot are similar to those of the layup shot, with the ball being carried to a position above the head before release. A player who fires the one-hand jump shot while moving obtains his spring from his left leg. But the player shooting from a stationary, or "set," position derives his spring from both legs.

When the shot is properly made the player "shoots it out of his left hand," with the right hand of course furnishing the impetus. Some players, however, remove the left hand earlier and the shot is more truly a one-hand move. As in the layup, the left hand protects the shot.

The fingers of the right hand are well spread behind the ball. The ball never is palmed. It is necessary for the shooter to obtain maximum height in order to shoot over the arms of the defender. Wrist and fingers supply the force necessary to push the ball to the basket. The back is straight. At the end of the shot the arm is fully extended in a follow-through motion. The head is up, the eyes focused on the center of the basket — not the rim, not the bankboard, but the center of the target.

A proper follow-through is necessary in this shot as in all shots. The player lands in either a parallel or stride position. We prefer the stride, because the player is better able to "shove off" and resume action.

Because the jump shot is released while the player is in the air, it is evident that his balance must be excellent. It is obvious also that this type of shot requires constant practice as well as a good shooting eye.

The two-hand set shot. This one has stood the test of time. It has lost some of its luster because of the rise in popularity of the one-hand shot, but it remains a valuable weapon. A good two-hand shooter, often operating from long range, is capable of changing the complexion of a game in a hurry. His work usually delights spectators — at least hometown spectators.

Players are permitted considerable leeway in the matter of foot position in this shot. Feet may be in the parallel or stride position or close together. However, the stride position is the most natural one for the feet of a player who has pivoted away from his guard.

Knees are slightly bent, body is tilted forward slightly, elbows are close to the body, and forearms are pointed slightly upward. The ball is controlled by fingers and thumbs and is held at about chin height. Back is straight, head up, and eyes focused on the center of the goal. In releasing the ball the player raises his arms in an upward and outward motion. Knees are straightened simultaneously. After the ball has left the fingertips arms are fully extended and palms face the direction of the shot. Body weight, equally distributed until the instant of the shot, is transferred to the toes and balls of the feet. The player steps forward slightly in the direction of the basket as he follows through.

The two-hand overhead shot. The two-hand overhead has become popular since the coming of the big man. It is essentially a big man's shot, released from a height that is out of reach of the defender. The mechanics are basically the same as in the two-hand set shot, except that the ball is carried to a two-hand position above the head. Finger position is the same, but thumbs are under the ball and directly over the shooter's head. Knees are bent slightly and the back is straight. Arms are bent at the elbows. Eyes are focused on the center of the basket.

When the shot is released the arms are fully extended. Wrists, fingers, and thumbs push the ball toward the goal. As in the two-hand set shot, the palms face the basket after the shot has been completed. In this shot, as in all shots, the player must refrain from following the flight of the ball with his eyes. His attention must be directed toward the target, and held there.

Foul shooting. Here again players may be given considerable leeway in adopting shooting styles. We just try to make the ball go into the basket. We do not change a player's style unless his score at the free line is distressingly low. We permit our players to shoot fouls in the same way that they shoot from the field, a common situation since the one-hand shot has become so popular. Good foul shooting becomes a habit, and a player wearing a blind fold, providing his shooting habits are sound, will shoot close to his normal percentage.

There is an emotional factor in foul shooting, of course, and players who seldom miss in practice often blow foul chances when the score is close. The coach can only hope for players with steady nerves. There is no shortcut to sound shooting habits. We practice foul shooting consistently and earnestly, shooting literally thousands of fouls in practice.

AN INTRODUCTION TO PASSING

We use only five types of passes. With these we feel that we can meet any situation that arises. We believe also that a player who has mastered the use of five passes is a better player than one who knows ten passes halfway.

As in shooting, we have a target in our passing: the receiver's chin. We have chosen that target because we have found that most passes tend to be low. By raising our target we usually hit the chest area, and it is from this area that most basketball maneuvers start.

We do not use overspin or backspin on any pass. We throw a "dead" ball because the spinning ball is difficult to handle. We throw the dead ball even in our bounce passes, since we have found that the spinning ball often is deflected from its course when it strikes the floor.

The two-hand chest pass. The two-hand chest pass may be thrown from any position. It is the ideal short pass but may be used for medium-length work in many situations, including the fast break, when passes are used instead of extensive dribbling. It is often used by guards advancing the ball or feeding players in the offensive court.

It is normally thrown from a stride position, since the player usually catches the ball while in that position. In most cases the knees are slightly bent and the body is tilted forward. Elbows are close to the body and forearms are nearly parallel to the floor. The ball is grasped firmly with fingers and thumbs. Head is up and the player surveys as much of the playing area as possible.

In releasing the ball, the player steps forward with his front foot in the direction of the pass receiver. Force is supplied by a quick extension of the arms and a final snap of wrists, fingers, and thumbs. Palms are pointed at the floor when the pass is completed.

The two-hand overhead pass. A pass more often used by the tall player, the two-hand overhead pass resembles the two-hand overhead shot. Instead of the basket, the target is a pass receiver. All mechanics are the same. The pass usually may be thrown without interference by the defender, because the ball is out of his reach. The passer steps forward and transfers the weight of his body to the front foot as the ball is thrown. The ball ordinarily follows a slightly downward path. Force is supplied by a forward movement of the arms and a snapping motion of wrists, fingers, and thumbs.

The two-hand bounce pass. Most often an offensive court pass, the two-hand bounce pass is used to get the ball from guard to forward, to the pivot man, from out of bounds under both baskets, or past a defender. It is usually executed from a stride position. Knees are slightly bent. The trunk is tilted slightly forward and weight is equally distributed. Elbows are close to the body. The ball is held firmly by fingers and thumbs about chest high. Head is up, back straight, and the player surveys the passing area.

In starting the pass, the player steps toward the receiver with his front foot. Arms are extended and the ball is aimed at a spot on the floor approximately three feet in front of the receiver. Enough force is applied by thumbs, fingers, and wrists to cause the ball to bounce roughly at belt height. Arms are extended fully and palms of the hands are facing the floor after the pass.

The one-hand bounce pass. This is a good close-in pass.

Its primary use is to get the ball to the pivot man. By means of this pass, the thrower may step away from his defender in such a manner that the latter may not interfere in any way.

Throwing this pass, the right-handed player steps to the side with his right foot. In making the stride he retains good body balance. Body weight is primarily on the right leg, which is bent at the knee. The left leg is reasonably straight. The ball is carried away from the defender and shoulder high, with both hands being used. The right hand is behind the ball and the fingers are well spread. The left hand steadies the ball. Both elbows are slightly bent. As the ball is released, the left hand is removed and the arm is extended to its full length. The ball is given its force by arm, wrist, fingers, and thumb. Properly thrown, the ball should strike a spot on the floor no more than three feet from the receiver and should bounce belt high.

The overhand baseball pass. A medium- or long-distance weapon, the baseball pass is most often used in launching a fast break. Feet are in a stride position. The ball is carried with both hands to a position within three or four inches of the right ear. Weight is on the right, or rear, leg. The body is tilted slightly backward and at an angle to the right. The fingers and thumb of the throwing hand are well spread and behind the ball. The head is up. As the pass is executed the left hand is removed from the ball and extended straight forward. This arm and hand protect the pass.

As the ball is brought forward the weight is transferred from the rear leg to the left, or front, leg and the body is rotated slightly until the passer faces the pass receiver. The right arm is brought forward as a baseball pitcher brings his arm forward. The last points of contact are the fingertips. When the ball is released the palm of the hand is parallel to the floor.

To obtain greater distance, the player has only to bring the ball back farther behind his head. The distance the ball is brought back will determine the length of the pass. The ball is thrown close to the passer's head in order to eliminate rotation of the hand, which causes the ball to curve.

Care should be taken to avoid use of too much force in this pass. No pass has value unless it can be handled by the receiver.

CATCHING THE BALL

Relaxation is the most important factor in catching the ball. The good player never fights the ball. He steps forward to meet the pass rather than waiting for it to come to him. This avoids interceptions. The feet, most often, are in a stride position when the ball is caught. Arms are extended toward the passer. Elbows are bent slightly; fingers and thumbs are well spread. The ball is caught in the fingers, with the butts, or heels, of the hands serving as cushions. The fingers are clamped on the ball immediately after contact is established. The arms, moving backward toward the body, help cushion the shock of the catch.

The player receiving a pass, like the player throwing the pass, must at all times keep his eyes on the ball. The receiver must be alert and prepared to reach for a poorly thrown pass or a pass that has been deflected.

THE DRIBBLE

Properly used, the dribble is a valuable part of offense. Improperly used, it damages the offense and turns an offensive player into an individualist who has forgotten the responsibilities of a good team player.

Dribbling usually is divided into two classifications, the "clever" dribble, used in a number of ways, and the "speed" dribble, normally employed by a player racing downcourt in the fast break.

The so-called clever dribble is used to move the ball from an overcrowded area, especially in starting the fast break. It is used to advance the ball against a pressing defense, to escape a defender who is guarding aggressively, and in normal ball advancement. The dribble often is used by a player waiting for teammates to set up an offensive maneuver. It may also be used to kill time, although recent rules changes have limited its use for this purpose. One of the most important uses of the dribble is in a straight drive toward the basket by a man who has avoided his defender.

In the clever dribble the feet are placed in a stride position, with the foot of the dribbling hand to the rear. Knees are bent, the body is tilted from the waist. The back is straight. The head is up. Eyes survey as much as possible of the playing area.

The fingers of the dribbling hand strike the top of the ball. The upper arm is perpendicular; the elbow is close to the body. The ball is controlled by the fingertips only. Enough force is applied to cause the ball to rebound smartly from the floor to the hand. There is little movement of the arm. The wrist and fingers provide rebounding force. The ball must not be pounded or slapped, but should be *pushed* to the floor. It is advantageous for a player to be able to alternate hands while dribbling. In this way he can often escape a guard. The good dribbler never looks at the ball, but watches *ahead* for a guard or a passing opportunity.

When, by means of the fake, the player has gained an

advantage over his defender and is ready to dribble past him, he drops his inside shoulder, places his body between the defender and the ball, and drives around him, dribbling low.

It is never wise to waste a dribbling opportunity by bouncing the ball once and then catching it. Players must also bear in mind that normally a well-thrown pass is more to be desired than the fanciest dribbling demonstration. Unwise use of the dribble slows the offense and destroys timing. Outstanding professional and college teams move the ball most often by means of good passing. They dribble sparingly.

The speed dribble differs from the clever dribble in the height of the rebound. In starting the speed dribble, the player pushes the ball out in front of him and runs after it. The rebound is at least waist high.

Obviously the height and general build of a player determines his dribbling form. It is wise for the coach to permit the player to dribble in the manner that suits him best, so long as he follows basic procedures.

FAKING

Faking may be done with or without the ball. The player with the ball fakes to get around the defender. The offensive player without the ball fakes to escape his guard and receive a pass. The defensive man fakes to force the offensive player to declare himself with a pass or dribble.

Basically, the fake is a feint designed to mask the true intention of the player using it. Faking is instinctive with the good player. He feints before passing, dribbling, and often before shooting. The entire body may be used to feint, although head, eyes, shoulders, arms, and feet may be used singly or in combination. Obviously many feints are made with the ball.

CUTTING

Cutting is primarily an offensive maneuver designed to enable the offensive player to rid himself of his guard. In executing a cut, the player strides with one foot, then reverses his direction, and, shoving off with the front foot, goes in the opposite direction past his guard.

In cutting the player employs the change of pace, the ability to stop, the quick start, the rear turn, and other body movements. Like faking, cutting must be well learned and practiced faithfully.

FUNDAMENTAL DRILLS

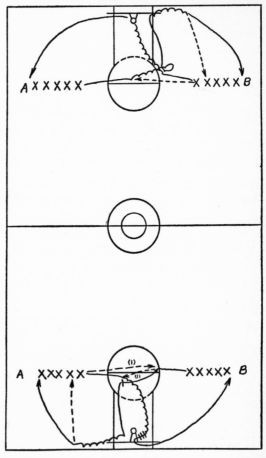

(Top.) *Line B passes to line A. A dribbles, executes a rear turn, and passes back to B. B dribbles in for layup shot. The feeder A rebounds, dribbles out, and passes to the next boy in line B. Each boy changes lines after the execution of the drill.*

(Bottom.) *Line A passes to line B. Line B immediately returns the pass to A; then B sets up a screen. A dribbles to basket off screen by B. B rebounds, passes to line A, and goes to the end of line A. The shooter A goes to the end of line B.*

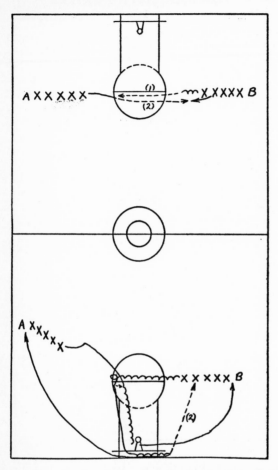

(Top.) *This is a passing drill, using the two-hand push pass, two-hand bounce pass, and one-hand layoff pass. During the drill we stress passing and catching techniques. The boys interchange lines. The drill should be started slow; then increase the speed of the drill. While executing the drill we do not stop.*

(Bottom.) *Line B dribbles and executes a rear turn. Line A fakes, drives, and receives the ball from B. A dribbles to the basket. B rebounds and passes to A. A, after shooting, goes to the rear of line B.*

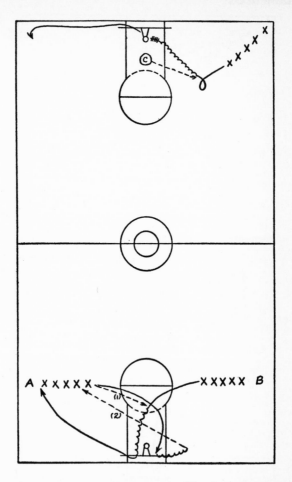

(Top.) *Boys line up as diagrammed. The front boy comes out, executes a rear turn, and receives a pass from © , the coach. He dribbles and shoots, then goes to the opposite corner. The drill is then executed from the opposite corner.*

(Bottom). *Line B cuts as diagrammed, receiving a pass from line A. Line B dribbles and shoots. A rebounds and passes to line A. B goes to the rear of line A. A goes to the rear of line B. This drill is good for teaching tight screening. Stress A cutting close to B.*

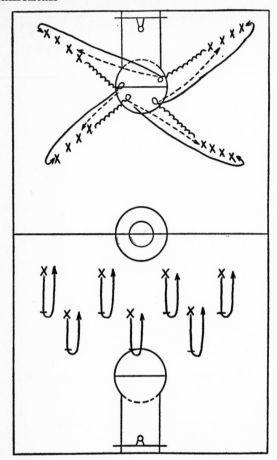

(Top.) *Rear turn drill. Start with two balls. The front boy dribbles out, executes a rear turn, and passes to the next line. Then he follows the pass and goes to the end of the line. After the boys have gone completely around, they reverse the pivot foot. To get some fun out of this drill, get them going and then on the whistle reverse the pivot foot, right to left or vice versa. Also use four balls.*

(Bottom.) *This is our "Rubber Ball Drill." The boys line up facing the center of the court. On the whistle each boy retreats, using a good defensive stance and slide. On the second whistle each boy falls to the floor, bounces back to a standing position, and then runs to his original starting position.*

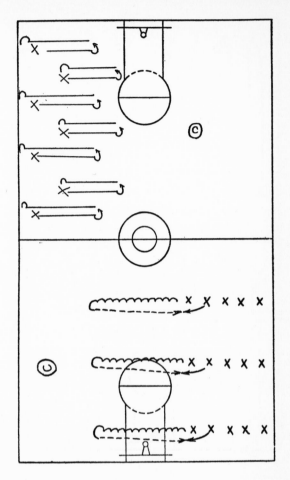

(Top.) *The boys line up. On the first whistle they run toward the coach, ©. On the second whistle each boy stops and executes a rear turn. In the beginning each boy holds his position, while the coach checks proper stance and balance. Later, on the second whistle, each boy executes a rear turn, runs back to his original starting place, and executes another rear turn.*

(Bottom.) *The first boy in each line dribbles forward, stops, executes a rear turn, and passes to the next boy. This drill is used for dribbling, passing, and following the pass.*

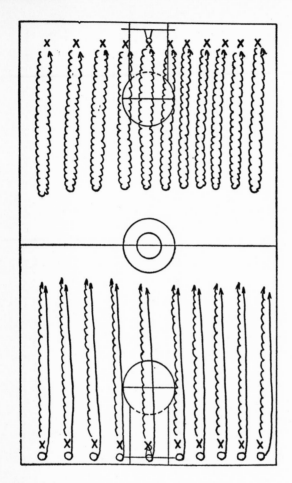

(Top.) *This is our "Go Home" drill. Each boy has a ball. On the first whistle he dribbles up the floor. On the second whistle he turns and dribbles rapidly to his starting position.*

(Bottom.) *Our "Dribble—Get Back on Defense" drill. X dribbles up the floor with O behind or beside him. When the coach blows the whistle, X puts the ball on the floor. O retrieves the ball and dribbles back to the baseline. X, in the meantime, has turned and assumed a defensive position. O dribbles fast to make X move fast. The distance to be dribbled up the court is optional.*

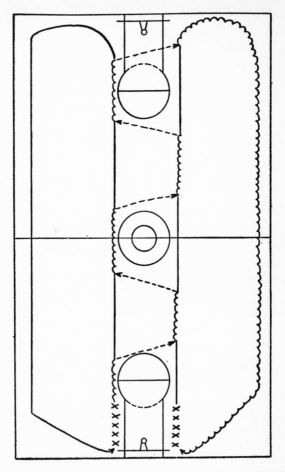

Two lines. Each pair of boys has a ball. The basic idea is to move the ball downcourt, passing between themselves. On each new or different pass, the boys walk at normal speed. As the drill progresses, the tempo of movement is speeded up. All types of passes are used in this drill. At the end of the shot, the boys peel off to their respective sides and return to their starting positions. Interchange lines. The boy with the ball dribbles back.

(Variation.) *Start one of the boys down fast. The opposite line throws a baseball pass at 20 feet, then follows the pass to catch up with or receive the ball back.*

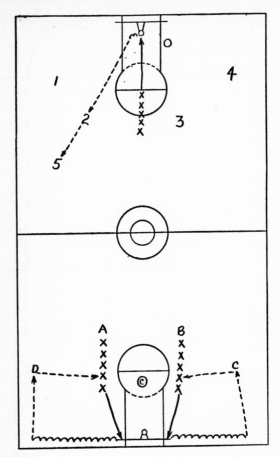

(Top.) O, *the coach, shoots; X rebounds; coach calls number (floor area) for the pass out. Call number before rebounder comes down, so he will think before starting his fake and drive to the sideline. As soon as 1, 2, 3, or 4 gets ball he passes to 5. At first, spot pass to 5; then let 5 roam. Rotate boys 5 to 4, etc. 1 goes to line X; X to 5 position.*

(Bottom.) ©, *the coach, has two balls. He shoots at board. Lines A and B rebound and dribble to their respective sides. B passes to C; C passes to front man in line B and then goes to rear of line. A passes to D; D passes to front man in line A and then goes to rear of line A. Stress good rebounding position, landing head and shoulder fake, ball protection, and low dribble. Interchange lines when drill is completed.*

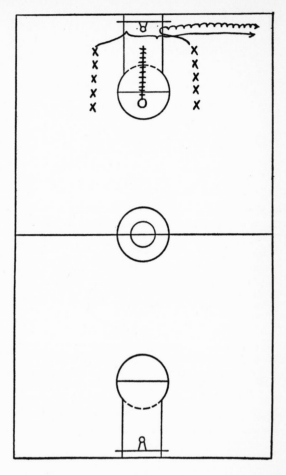

O *shoots and lines* A *and* B *rebound. Whichever boy gets the rebound is on offense. The other boy is on defense. It is up to the offensive boy to get free from the defensive man.*

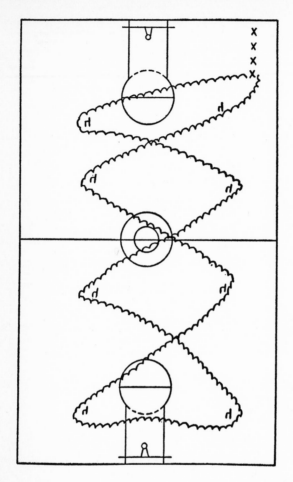

Dribble straight at the chair with the left hand. On reaching the chair switch the ball to the right hand. Dribble to next chair with the right hand, then switch to left hand. Another switching drill consists of alternating the left and right hands with every bounce of the ball.

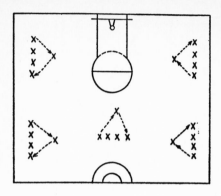

(Left.) *Our "Pepper Drill." Boys line up as diagrammed. Two balls are used. This is a good drill for helping a boy improve his split vision.*

(Right.) *Two lines. ©, the coach, demonstrates each type of pass. The boys execute the pass and the coach corrects them. Start about 6 feet apart, then increase the distance for the pass.*

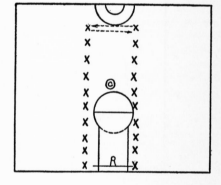

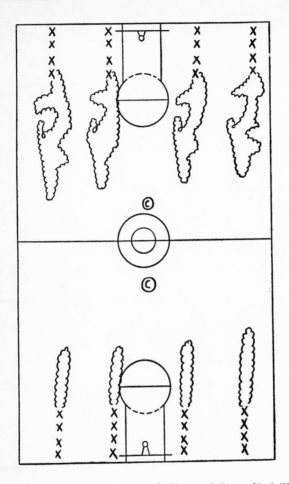

(Top.) *This is our "Stop, Go, Back Up, and Lateral" drill. The boys are down on one knee to start the drill. On each whistle, watching the coach, the boys execute the drill according to the way the coach indicates he is going to dribble.*

(Bottom.) *This is our checking drill for dribbling. Each boy is dribbling a ball, with one knee on the floor. As the boys are dribbling, ©, the coach, checks their form, making the necessary corrections. Then each boy dribbles as shown. Start the drill slowly, then speed it up.*

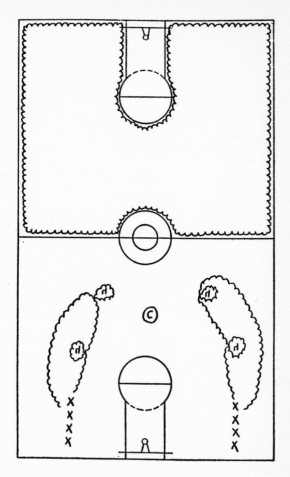

(Top.) *In this drill, we dribble the lines of the court as indicated. This is a good competitive drill.*

(Bottom.) *The boys dribble up to and around the chairs. After dribbling around the last chair, each boy peels off to his respective side and dribbles for speed to his starting position. The number of chairs is optional.*

● The offense

BASKETBALL OFFENSE, STRIPPED OF ITS FRILLS, BECOMES a six-word admonition: *Get the ball in the basket!* Every move by every man engaged in the attack is designed to make possible a shot that, if properly aimed and helped on its way by reasonably friendly gremlins, will drop neatly into the nets, causing wheels to turn in scoreboard mechanisms and hope to bloom afresh in the hearts of coaches.

Obviously these shots and field baskets are hard to come by, due to the fact that earnest defenders are ready, yea, eager, to suffer the torment of floorburn and Charley horse to thwart the offensive thrust. They are also eager, those five pestiferous defenders, to sieze the basketball and stuff it into the other basket.

The basic task of the offense is to outwit the defense. By means of blocks and screens, by employing speed and the element of surprise, by utilizing its skill in dribbling and passing, by the use of all the deception at its command, the offense seeks to force the defense to fail in its task. As the football offense must carry the ball past the goal line, the basketball offense must advance the ball to a point from which a shot is feasible, arrange to obtain that shot, and hit it. Simple? Of course it's simple. That's why most coaches have gray hair!

It is often possible for the skillful player to make his own scoring opportunities. This kind of basketball, usually called the free-lance game, is effective when it is a part—and only a part—of an offense whose main strength is in team effort. Individual initiative is wholesome so long as it does not become glory-grabbing, and all members of the team must be ready to assist an individual in exploiting his personal skill and initiative. It is the task of the coach to develop patterns that will best afford opportunities for players to utilize their desire to score. He must teach them the proper methods of turning certain situations to their advantage.

In the free-lance game options are many, and the good free-lance player is equipped to select the proper maneuver from a large and varied supply. It is this type of offense that we employ at Muncie Central. In teaching the free-lance offense we first set up the pattern and then demonstrate a few play options, which are "walked through" to make them more easily understood. We use no more than ten options, and the position of the ball and movements of the players determine the option to be used in a particular situation. Although the system includes a few "tips," or signals, as to option selection, we expect our players to be able to fit the proper option to unfolding situations. All play in this offense must have continuity. All options are set for one side of the floor but may also be used on the other.

Guards and forwards must be able to interchange positions, although the pivot man remains in his own area. Our offense is so arranged that, if all players carry out their assignments properly, we will have at least two players ready to rebound under the offensive board.

We do not hesitate to shoot, and operate on the theory that any player who is within ten feet of the basket and who has a fifty-fifty chance of getting a shot away is to take that shot. We do not take bad shots, since we are confident that our pattern, properly followed, will produce good shots. We do not, however, become so hidebound in our play that we pass up a good shot if one comes our way by accident. Some coaches appear to have the idea that the ball must be passed a half-dozen times before a shot can be turned loose. We shoot when the shot is there. The main idea still is to get the ball into that net.

We start our offensive drilling with one-man options in which it is the duty of one offensive man to use all his basketball knowledge and physical ability to escape from one guard. The next step is to insert another man and the two-man option is in operation. The guard may pass to the forward and the forward back to the guard, who has cut outside. The guard then may dribble or shoot. The guard may pass to the forward and use an inside screen. The forward in turn may dribble off the screen for a shot. If there is a defensive shift, the guard may roll out of the screen for a return pass from the forward. The guard may signal the forward to screen his defensive man, after which he may drive off the screen for a shot. If there is a defensive switch, the forward may roll out of his screen for a return pass from the guard.

It should be explained here that the terms "screen," "block," and "pick" mean essentially the same thing. They are all maneuvers by means of which one offensive man uses a teammate to free himself from his defender. In all cases the man screening, blocking, or picking places his body between that of his teammate and the defender, and in legal fashion.

Rules make it clear that the offensive blocker must give the defensive man enough room to move in any direction. It is not permissible for the blocker to jump all over the defender the way a football end checks a defensive half-back to clear the way for a carrier. The blocker must not move after having established his position.

To be effective, a pick or block must be executed with the entire body, front or back. A pick made with the side of the body is only half as effective. When the pick or block has been established it is the duty of the offensive man with the ball to cause his defender to run into the blind switch set up by the block. The offensive player using a teammate as a blocker must pass close to the block to make it impossible for the defensive man to move through the block with him. He must avoid use of the loop, or circle, in rounding a block, since the defender then is given ample room to move past and the block becomes worthless.

The word "screen," in addition to its use for a block or a pick, applies also to a maneuver in which an offensive player pauses long enough for a teammate to shoot from behind him, thus "screening" him from the defender.

After the two-man option has been learned, we add a third man: the pivot man. In this setup the ball is thrown to the pivot man and we are ready to utilize our three-man options, all of which are diagrammed in this chapter. The pivot man has a number of choices. He may shoot or give back to the cutting forward, who has cut in front of him, or to the guard, who has continued to drive toward the basket along the endline.

In our system the fourth player is the other guard. This player may use the forward for a screen in his cut to the basket. In such an option our signal tells the first guard to roll out to the corner. The fifth player, the other forward, moves out to a defensive position in case of an error. The first guard, in rolling out of the corner, comes back fast to get into the defensive picture if defense becomes necessary. If nothing materializes, we start all over, although we normally are able to obtain a good shot when the pattern is followed properly. Our system is designed to offer a great number of scoring opportunities, but these may be exploited only if every player carries out his assignments to give the pattern continuity.

The starting position of the thrust is determined by the first forward to handle the ball. If he ignores the cutting guard and passes back to the other guard, this guard starts the options on the other side of the floor. When this takes place a guard becomes a forward and a forward a guard, which makes plain the need for knowledge of both positions.

In choosing the offensive style, most coaches have a tendency to lean toward the style in which they themselves were schooled. Other coaches change as often as the weather. Along that line, coaches should bear in mind that it is the material that makes a system work or causes it to fail. Nobody but Merlin could make a racehorse out of a plowhorse. A system that wins on paper may not win on game night. The system that produced victories last year may not work with the personnel available this year.

But the coach must start somewhere, and it is wise to adopt a system early in the year, work out offensive and defensive patterns, and give the system a fair chance to work. The system should be simple enough that every player can understand it. Starters should be chosen as early as possible.

There are coaches who change their systems when their teams lose two games in a row. Although there are times when a system must be forsaken, the coach should be certain that the system is at fault before he makes a change. Some coaches, having watched a college team win an easy victory, hasten home to install its system on their own courts. Obviously this won't work often because the high school coach is limited by the skill, or lack of skill, of players younger than those at the college level. College coaches handpick players who fit into their particular systems. High school coaches cannot do this.

The free-lance offense has a flexibility that keeps defenders guessing. It gives players mobility and, because it permits them to think for themselves, makes the game more pleasant to play. It has proved popular with patrons. It produces a great number of good shots and no coach can ask for more than that. Most important of all, the free-lance system wins basketball games.

Diagrams presented with this chapter are designed to explain our offensive system. It has worked for us; it can work for others.

THE SEMI-CONTROL GAME

A number of prep coaches, because they like it personally or because it fits their material, send out teams equipped with the offense generally known as the semi-control, or strict pattern, game. Built on only four or five options, it is simple and foolproof and often fills the requirements of the coach who has no towering pivot man. The ball usually is put in play from the right side of the court and the uncomplicated pattern is run through and repeated until the team obtains the shot it desires. There is no hurried shooting, and, if the defense is napping, its system of careful blocks produces good scoring opportunities. Properly handled, it is a formidable offense no matter how alert the defense.

The semi-control game is based on the old system in which the center screens to the opposite side of the ball so that the opposite forward can cut across the foul circle. Its first option is identical to that of the free-lance offense, with the guard passing to the forward and then cutting outside him. If nothing develops between the guard and the forward or the pivot man, the pivot moves opposite the ball to block for the opposite forward and then rolls to the baseline. If the forward who has the ball does not pass to the cutting forward, he feeds it out to the other guard.

As the guard receives the ball, the pivot man moves from the baseline to a position where the foul line meets the foul circle. The guard then maneuvers in such a manner as to use the pivot man as a blocker for his own drive. As a variation, the guard may pass to the pivot man, then cut by him for a return pass. The pivot man himself may shoot, or, if this is impossible, he may pass out and the pattern is repeated.

To make the semi-control offense work all players must be good ball-handlers. They must be patient. Many high school players tend to fire a bad shot if a good one fails to materialize. The semi-control game is based on strict ball control and shots must be taken only at the time and place of the offensive team's choosing. This attack, although it does not often produce large scores, usually enables a team to hold down the score of its opponent because the opponent has the ball less often. For this reason it is often good against a foe who is much stronger offensively. Diagrams of this attack are included in this chapter.

ATTACKING THE ZONE

Here are a few good rules to remember in operating against the zone defense:

DRIBBLE ONLY WHEN ABSOLUTELY NECESSARY.

USE SHARP, ACCURATE PASSES—THE BOUNCE PASS IN CLOSE QUARTERS AND THE TWO-HAND CHEST PASS ON THE OUTSIDE.

PASS QUICKLY TO KEEP DEFENDERS MOVING.

DON'T BE IN A HURRY—TAKE GOOD SHOTS.

FOLLOW A DEFINITE PLAN AND MAKE YOUR PATTERN WORK.

Don't let the zone frighten you. Go after it. Don't admit defeat by holding the ball, even if you are ahead. You gained your lead by attacking. Attack again. Move into the offense quickly to prevent the defense from forming a zone. Play common-sense basketball, especially near the end of the game.

In attacking the zone, we use the 1-3-1 offense and have found it successful in most cases. Although we encounter few zones, our players always are taught to attack it. We are partial to the 1-3-1 attack because it gives better floor balance and is easy to teach. The pattern has continuity. We have never yet failed to get good shots against a zone by following this plan.

FUNDAMENTAL DRILLS IN OFFENSE-BUILDING

We build our offense on an individual basis. Diagrams that accompany this chapter show our offense as we teach it each year. Defense is not taught when offensive work begins but is added after two weeks. Each player except the pivot man is required to execute the drills from each position, enabling him to become familiar with every situation that might arise. Our pivot man operates solely in the pivot area. Three players work in the pivot after we begin using that position. Otherwise the pivot works in all two-man drills. We use both ends of the floor. The assistant coach takes one end, the head coach the other.

Two-man drills, shown in the diagrams on pages 77 to 79, are for guard and forward play on the side of the floor. The diagrams on pages 80 to 82 show our two-man drills from guard to guard.

Three-man drills appear in the diagrams on pages 82 to 86. They are for guard, forward, and pivot play on the side of the floor. In all drills *X3*, the pivot man, is in position to receive a pass, shoot, set a block, or rebound. The three-man drills in the diagrams on pages 87 to 89 are for guard, forward, and guard.

The four-man drills (shown in the diagrams on pages 89 to 92) involve the guards, a forward, and the pivot man.

All these drills are practiced from both sides of the floor. Play of the fifth man is shown in the diagrams on pages 93 and 94. In our offense he is a free-lancer, the first to sense and take advantage of a situation. He is a rebounder. If he sees that we have good rebounding position, he becomes a safety valve for defense. If the ball is brought back to his side of the floor, this maneuver being determined by the first forward to handle the ball, our fifth man becomes a part of the options on his side of the floor.

In drills involving two or more players we stress (*1*) the necessity of cutting close to all blocks, (*2*) accurate ball-handling and good dribbling, (*3*) proper footwork and good body position, and (*4*) the necessity of carrying out the option to the end.

Diagrams on pages 94 and 95 show out-of-bounds plays from the side of the court and under the basket. The diagram at the bottom of page 95 is one of our "specials" for use after a time-out or at the start of a period. The diagrams on pages 96 to 98 deal with the attack on the zone. Diagrams on pages 98 and 99 illustrate the semi-control game.

BUILDING THE OFFENSE

(Right.) *Fake once and drive for a layup shot. Fake twice and drive for a layup shot. Fake a shot, fake a drive, then drive for a layup shot. Repeat, using jump shot. Shooter goes to next numbered position. Two balls may be used to speed up the practice. No defense is used.*

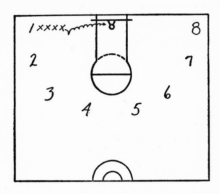

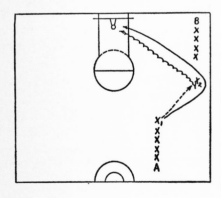

(Left.) *X1 passes to X2 and follows his pass. X2 fakes a return pass to X1 and then dribbles in for a shot. X1 rebounds, passes to line A, and goes to line B. X2 goes to line A. The passes used are two-hand chest pass, two-hand bounce pass, one-hand bounce pass, and two-hand overhead pass. The rebounder passing to line A uses one-hand baseball pass.*

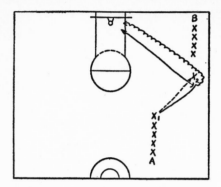

(Left.) X1 *passes to X2 and follows his pass. X2 hands off to X1. X1 dribbles in for a layup. X2 rebounds, passes to line A, and then goes to line A. X1 goes to line B.*

(Right.) X1 *passes to X2. X2 passes back and uses body for block. X1 dribbles off block for layup. As soon as X1 is past, X2 rebounds, passes to line A, and goes to line A. X1, after shooting, goes to line B.*

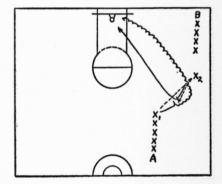

(Right.) X2 *comes out and forms a block for* X1. X1 *dribbles in for layup.* X2 *follows in for a rebound, passes to line* A, *and goes to line* A. X1, *after shooting, goes to line* B. *Stress proper blocking form (with front of body).*

(Option.) X1 *passes back to* X2 *coming out of block.* X2 *then shoots, with* X1 *rebounding and passing out to line* A.

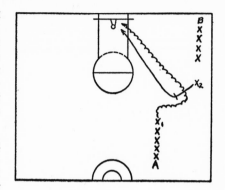

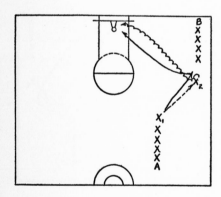

(Left.) X1 *passes to* X2 *and sets an inside block.* X2 *dribbles off block for shot.* X1 *follows for rebound, passes to line* A, *and goes to line* B. X2, *after shooting, goes to line* A.

TWO-MAN DRILLS FROM GUARD POSITION

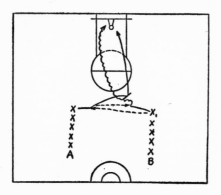

(Left). X1 *passes to X2. X2 gives back to X1 and X1 dribbles in for shot. X2 goes for rebound, passes to line B, and then goes to line B. X1 goes to line A.*

(Option.) X2 *fakes pass to X1. X2 dribbles in for shot. X1 rebounds.*

(Right.) X1 *passes to X2 and sets block. X2 dribbles off block for shot. X1 comes out of block to rebound, passes to line B, and goes to line A. X2 goes to line B.*

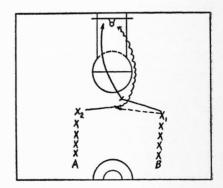

(Right.) X1 *passes to X2. X2 returns pass and sets block. X1 dribbles off block for shot. X2 rebounds, passes to line B, and goes to line B. X1 goes to line A.*

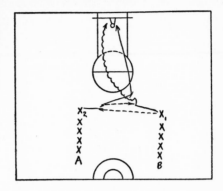

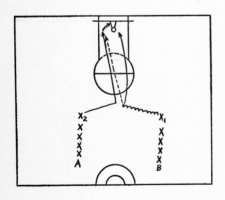

(Left.) *X2 comes across and fakes a block. X1 dribbles, then passes to X2, using a lead pass. X2 shoots and goes to line B. X1 rebounds, passes to line B, and goes to line A.*

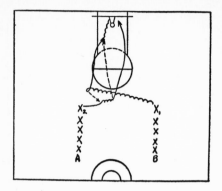

(Left.) X1 *dribbles hard at X2 and flips the ball to him. He then breaks to the basket and receives a pass from X2. X1 shoots and goes to line A. X2 rebounds, passes to line B, and goes to line B.*

THREE-MAN DRILLS:
GUARD, FORWARD, AND PIVOT

(Right.) X1 *passes to X2 and goes outside. X2 passes to X3 and cuts. X3 passes to either X1 or X2. X3 rebounds and passes to line A. X1 goes to line B. X2 goes to line A. In all these three-man drills X3 may pass either to X1 or X2.*

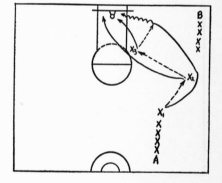

(Right.) X1 *passes to X2.*
X2 hands back to X1. X1
dribbles in for shot. X2
cuts to basket. X3 re-
bounds and passes to line
A. X1 goes to line B, and
X2 goes to line A.

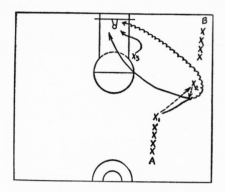

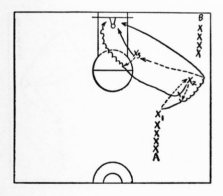

(Left.) X1 *passes to X2,*
who returns a fast pass to
X1 and then sets block.
X1 dribbles, passes to X3,
and cuts. X2 cuts from
block. X3 hands off to X2,
who shoots. X3 rebounds
and passes to line A. X1
goes to line B. X2 goes
to line A.

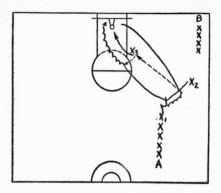

(Left.) X2 *comes out and sets block. X1 dribbles off block, passes to X3, and cuts. X2 fades from block. X3 hands off to X2, who shoots. X3 rebounds and passes to line A. X2 goes to line A. X1 goes to line B.*

(Right.) X2 *comes out and sets block. X1 dribbles off block. X3 sets block for X1. X1 dribbles in for shot. X2 and X3 fade from blocks. X3 rebounds and passes to line A. X1 goes to line B. X2 goes to line A.*

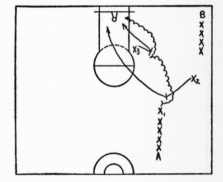

(Right.) X1 *passes to X2 and then sets an inside screen. X2 dribbles, passes to X3, and cuts. X1 rolls from block. X3 feeds X1, who shoots. X3 rebounds and passes to line A. X1 goes to line B. X2 goes to line A.*

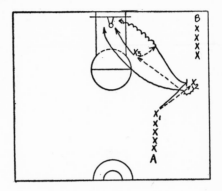

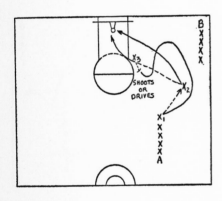

(Left.) X1 *passes to X2 and goes to outside. X2 passes to X3 and cuts to X3's left. X1 then comes around behind X2. X3 feeds X1, who shoots or drives. X3 rebounds and passes to line A. X1 goes to line B. X2 goes to line A.*

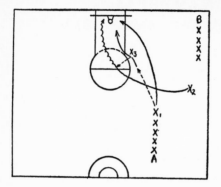

(Left.)   X1 *passes to X3 and cuts to same side. X2 cuts off* X1. X3 *passes to* X2, *who shoots. X3 rebounds and passes to line* A. X2 *goes to line* A *and* X1 *goes to line* B.

(Right.)   X1 *passes to* X2, *who passes quickly to* X3. X2 *cuts and* X1 *cuts close.* X3 *passes to* X1, *rebounds, and passes to line* A. X1 *goes to line* B *and* X2 *goes to line* A.

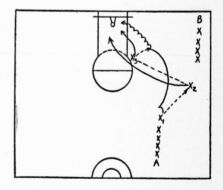

THREE-MAN DRILLS:
GUARD, FORWARD, AND GUARD

(Right.) X1 *passes to* X2 *and sets a block for* X4. X2 *passes to* X4 *and cuts.* X4 *dribbles and shoots.* X1 *rolls out of block, rebounds, and passes to line* B. *Players rotate:* X4 *to line* C, X1 *to line* A, *and* X2 *to line* B.

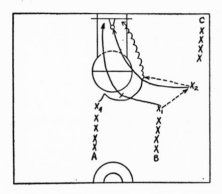

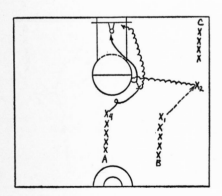

(Left.) X1 *passes to* X2 *and goes outside.* X2 *dribbles and hands off to* X4, *who dribbles and shoots.* X2 *rebounds and passes to line* B. *Players rotate:* X4 *to line* C, X1 *to line* A, *and* X2 *to line* B.

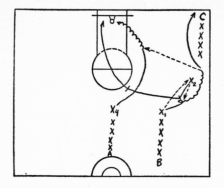

(Left.) X1 *passes to X2, who quickly returns the pass and blocks. After X1 has gone by, X2 sets block for X4. X1 passes to X4, who shoots. X2 rebounds and passes to line B. Players rotate: X4 to line C, X1 to line A, and X2 to line B.*

(Right.) X1 *passes to X2, then blocks for X4. X2 dribbles across and passes to X4, who dribbles and shoots. This is a double pick play. X2 rebounds and passes to line B. Players rotate: X4 to line C, X1 to line A, and X2 to line B.*

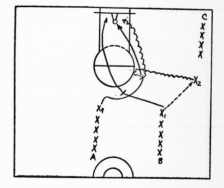

(Right.) X4 *dribbles around block set by* X1 *and passes to* X2. X2 *passes to* X1, *who rolls out of block.* X2 *rebounds and passes to line* A. *Players rotate:* X4 *to line* C, X1 *to line* A, *and* X2 *to line* B.

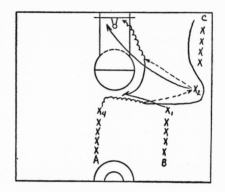

FOUR-MAN DRILLS:
GUARD, FORWARD, PIVOT, AND GUARD

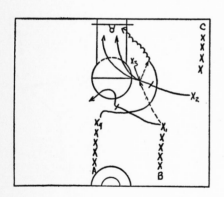

(Left.) X1 *passes to* X3 *and sets block for* X4. X2 *sets another block for* X4, *who uses both blocks.* X3 *passes to* X4, *who shoots.* X2 *rebounds and passes to line* B. *Players rotate:* X1 *to line* A, X2 *to line* B, *and* X4 *to line* C.

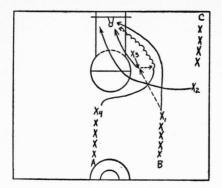

(Left.) X1 *passes to X3
and cuts. X2 cuts close
to X1. X4 cuts off X2. X3
feeds X4, who shoots. X2
rebounds and passes to line
B. Players rotate: X1 to
line A, X2 to line B, and
X4 to line C.*

(Right.) X1 *passes to X3,
then cuts. X4 cuts off X1.
X2 cuts off X4. X3 passes
to X2, who shoots. X1 re-
bounds and passes to line
B. Players rotate: X1 to
line A, X2 to line B, and
X4 to line C.*

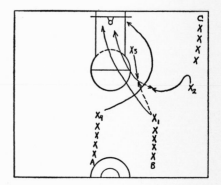

(Right.) X1 *dribbles to-*
ward X4 and hands ball
to him. X4 dribbles and
passes to X2, who passes to
X3 and then cuts. X1 rolls
out close to X2. X3 passes
to X1, who shoots. X3 re-
bounds and passes to line
B. Players rotate: X1 to
line A, X2 to line B, X4
to line C.

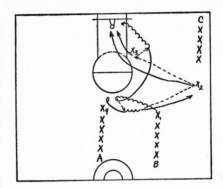

(Option.) X2 *keeps ball,*
dribbles, and then passes
to X1, who rolls off him.
X3 may set block.

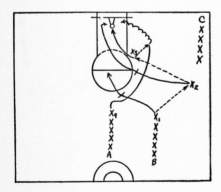

(Left.) X1 *passes to X2,*
then sets block for X4. X2
passes to X3 and sets
block. X4 cuts off blocks
set by X1 and X2. X3
passes to X4, who shoots.
X2 rebounds and passes to
line B. Players rotate: X1
to line A, X2 to line B,
and X4 to line C.

(Options.) X1 *may also*
pass to X4 and then set a
block. X4 may dribble off
block. X2 and X3 may
also set a block. Thus a
triple block is set for X4,
who maneuvers for a shot.

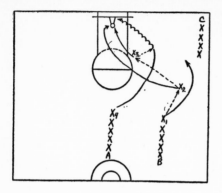

(Left.) X1 *passes to X2 and goes outside. X2 passes to X3 and cuts. X4 cuts off X2. X3 feeds X4, who shoots. X3 rebounds and passes to line B. Players rotate: X1 to line A, X2 to line B, and X4 to line C.*

(Right.) X4 *passes to X1, then blocks. X1 fakes to block, then passes to X2. X2 passes to X3 and cuts. X4 rolls out of block and cuts off X2. X3 passes to X4, who shoots. X3 rebounds and passes to line A. Players rotate: X1 to line A, X2 to line B, and X4 to line C.*

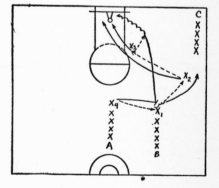

MOVEMENTS OF OTHER FORWARD, X5, IN PATTERN

(Right.) *This option is diagrammed to show how X5 operates in the pattern. When this option is set up,* X4, *after shooting, follows on through, coming out for defense.* X1 *rolls out and back for defense.* X2 *rebounds to weak side.* X3 *rolls with his pass and rebounds the strong side.* X5 *fills in in front of basket for rebound. On some options* X5 *rebounds the weak side.*

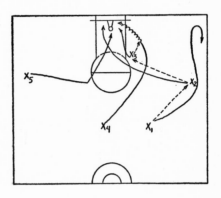

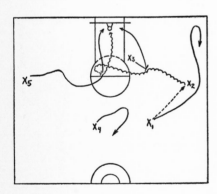

(Left.) *This option shows possible movement of* X5 *if* X2 *is stopped during his dribble.* X1 *passes to* X2 *and goes outside.* X2 *dribbles.* X3 *sets block and* X2 *is stopped.* X5 *moves out as usual, then cuts, taking pass from* X2. X5 *shoots.* X3 *rolls from block and rebounds right side.* X2 *follows pass and rebounds left side.* X1 *rolls to outside and comes back on defense.* X4 *stays back after seeing his option disappear.* X5 *may also set block for* X2 *in foul circle.*

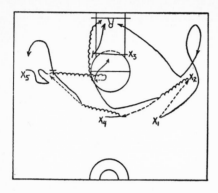

(Left.) *This diagram shows how X5 and X1 operate when ball is passed back to X4 and that player takes ball to opposite side and passes to X5. Note interchange of positions between X1 and X2, as well as movement of X5. Floor balance is important. X1 passes to X2 and goes outside. X4 moves across. X2 dribbles and passes to X4. As X5 sees this he returns to original position.* X4 *then passes to X5 and sets inside block. X5 dribbles off the block to foul line. X2, who has followed his pass to X4, cuts to receive pass from X5. X3 moves across to block for X2. X2 dribbles in for shot. Note movements of X1 from forward position. X4 rolls out of block for defense.*

OUT-OF-BOUNDS OPTIONS:
SIDE AND UNDER BASKET

(Right.) X2 *passes to X3 and cuts. X1 cuts close to X2. X3 passes to either player. X2 rebounds left side. X3 rolls with pass and rebounds right side. X5 moves across and rebounds front area. X4 stays back on defense.*

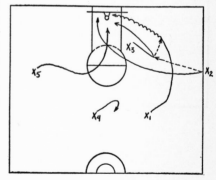

(Right.) *Out-of-bounds option under basket. X2 sets block for X5. X5 cuts. X2 rolls out of block. X3 passes to either player.*

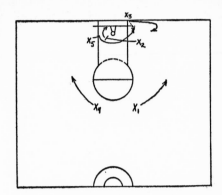

ONE OF OUR SPECIALS

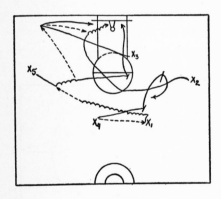

(Left.) *X4 passes to X1 and sets block. X1 dribbles and passes to X5. X5 starts dribble and passes to X3, who has gone to corner. X4 rolls out of block for X1 and sets block for X2. X2 cuts off block. X5, after passing to X3, moves across and sets another block for X2. X2 uses this block. X3 passes to X2, who shoots. X3 rebounds left side. X5 rolls from block and rebounds right side. X4 fills in from block to foul circle. X1 stays back on defense.*

ATTACKING THE ZONE

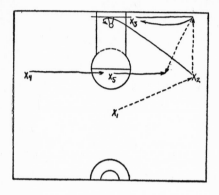

(Left, Basic Pattern.) X1 *passes to X2. X2 passes to X3. X2 cuts. X5 moves as indicated after X2 cuts. X4 replaces X5. X3 has three options. He may shoot, pass to X2, or pass to X5. As soon as X3 declares, he follows to basket. X5 has two options. He may shoot or pass to X4. X5 holds until X4 declares. If X4 cannot do anything, he passes back to X1. X1 starts over. Note new positions of players.*

(Right.) *Options are the same as in the preceding diagram.*

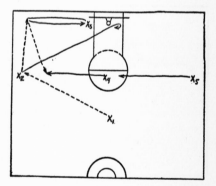

(Right.) X1 *dribbles, then bounce passes to X5. X5 passes to X2, who passes to X3 and cuts. X5 moves as indicated after X2 cuts. X4 replaces X5. X3 passes to X5, who shoots. X2, X3, and X4 rebound.*

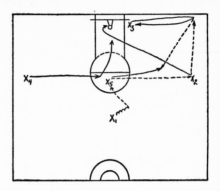

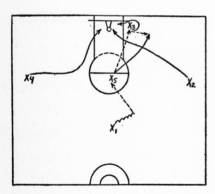

(Left.) X1 *dribbles and bounce passes to X5. X5 is alert to pass to X3, who shoots if possible. X2 cuts. X5 cuts off X2 as indicated. X3 passes to X5, who shoots. Note movement of X4. X2, X3, and X4 rebound.*

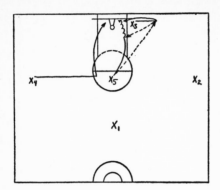

(Left.) X1 *dribbles and bounce passes to X5. X5 passes to X3 and cuts down foul lane to take return pass from X3. X4 and X3 rebound.*

THE SEMI-CONTROL GAME

(Right, Basic Pattern.) X1 *passes to X2. X2 waits until X1 is past. X3 goes to baseline. X5 cuts through foul circle. X2 passes to X5, who shoots. X2 and X3 rebound. X1 comes out for defense. The next diagram shows how ball is returned to X4.*

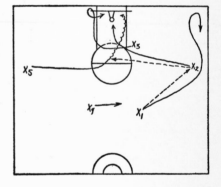

(Right.) X2 *passes back out to* X4. *X3 comes to position at which foul line bisects foul circle.* X4 *uses* X3 *for block.* X4 *may dribble off* X3's *block or pass to* X3 *and cut by for return pass.* X2, X3, *and* X5 *rebound.* X1 *comes out for defense.* X4 *rolls out after shot for defense.*

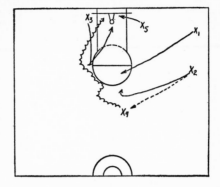

six

• The fast-breaking offense

NATHAN BEDFORD FORREST, AN EXCELLENT FAST-BREAK man, said it first: "Get thar fustest with the most-est!" Correctly employed, the fast-breaking offense is a useful, reliable, often devastating weapon. It is not, however, a shotgun blast fired by a man who has closed both eyes. Neither is it a magic wand that never fails to produce points and victories.

The fast-breaking offense is more than a helter-skelter rush downcourt. It is a carefully planned, skillfully executed maneuver that requires as much coaching effort as any other phase of the offense or defense.

Because of its great importance in modern basketball,

100

the fast-breaking offense is being covered in this separate chapter, rather than as a part of the regular offense. It is necessary that players know thoroughly the specific aims of this offense. They must be aware of the need for split-second timing and perfect team coordination. They must be taught that failure of one player to carry out his assignment not only may wreck a particular thrust, but may result in an enemy score, since the fast break usually commits a team wholly and affords it little possibility of orderly retreat.

Constant practice and familiarity with fast-break situations are of great importance. Once a coach called time-out and then sent his team back into action with orders to use a fast-break pattern it had never practiced. The result was chaos. Some coaches and many spectators believe the fast break consists of a pell-mell dash downcourt after an opponent has missed a field goal attempt. It isn't quite that simple. An occasional "cheap" basket may result from such a scramble, but usually the team pays dearly for an ill-conceived, poorly executed fast-break thrust.

Stripped to its essentials, the fast break is an attempt by the offensive team to flood the offensive court with more players than the defense can muster in that particular area. The offense then may profit by the situations known as the two-on-one, three-on-two, four-on-three, and even five-on-four. Most often the ratio is two-on-one or three-on-two.

It is plain that efficiency in certain fundamentals must be obtained if the fast-break offense is to be utilized. Drills in these skills must be an important part of the practice routine.

Most fast-break situations develop quickly and it is the duty of every player to be ready to take advantage of them. Players must know when to dribble, when to pass, and to whom. Either movement must be executed with confidence and precision. Many fast-break situations develop when the opponent errs — players must react swiftly in order to capitalize on these misplays.

The fast break is a worthwhile maneuver whenever a team obtains possession of the ball and is convinced that it can outnumber the enemy in a quick drive. The team must be what coaches term "fast-break conscious" and must be made to feel that the fast-break gamble is well worth taking. It can always slow its drive if the defense gets back.

A winning team is constantly alert for fast-break possibilities. If the chances for success are 60 per cent or better, or if a team outnumbers the opposition in any combination, it should go — and go fast. It should not, however, fast break blindly. And if it sees that the percentage scales have tipped against it, it should change smoothly to its usual offensive pattern.

PULLING THE TRIGGER

At the very beginning, if the fast break is to be successful, the ball must be moved out of the backcourt adroitly. The thrust usually fails if any player neglects to take his proper position in the fast-break pattern. Players must react swiftly and start quickly. The ball, whether thrown or dribbled, must be moved forward if possible. No good player involved in a fast break passes to a man behind him unless forced to do so.

Most fast-break possibilities are born when field or foul goals are missed, passes are intercepted, the ball is obtained from a jump ball, or a floor violation takes place. When the latter situation develops, the nearest player hustles out of bounds for the throw-in and other players, reacting quickly, break for the basket. When the ball is obtained players must move to their proper areas quickly to give the man with the ball a passing target. The first pass is the big pass in the fast break.

As the ball rebounds, after a missed field goal attempt, players in that area must go after it. The rebounder goes up with his body in the spread position and reaches his maximum height, arms spread, as the ball starts down. When he obtains possession he grasps the ball firmly and comes down with feet well spread for good balance. Head and shoulder fakes are useful in clearing "working room," although it may be necessary for him to dribble toward the sideline. The rebounder must ever be alert for a pass receiver. If one is in sight, he passes to him and breaks for the offensive court, although he may also become the trailer in the play.

If there is no receiver uncovered, the rebounder begins the fast break by dribbling, although he must not fail to pass to the first open man who is ahead of him. If the opposing center is slow to get back, the rebounder may dribble without hesitation through the middle of the court. In this case outside men remain near the sidelines as they move downcourt.

Occasionally players who are behind the ball neglect to drive, believing they are out of the play and of no value to the break. This is incorrect, since the front man may meet resistance and be forced to wheel and pass to a trailing player. The latter also may be in position to rebound a missed field goal attempt if he is driving hard.

Generally, our teams follow definite patterns in the execution of the fast break. (See diagrams at the end of this chapter.) Obviously, the formations are governed by the positions of defensive players, although we go straight in when we are able to get behind the defense. The natural equipment of high school boys rarely includes all the fast-break skills, and patient coaching is necessary to teach them to select and retain proper lanes, to move into open areas, and to receive and throw passes properly.

In exploiting the fast break it is important to get the ball to the middleman as quickly as possible, since, if he reaches an open area, he is in position to see the entire court and to pick passing targets. If the dribbler is ahead of his mates, he moves to the middle automatically, where he dribbles until he meets opposition. On reaching the foul circle, the dribbler may slacken his pace briefly to permit players on the side to make their cuts. If the guard retreats, he continues to dribble in for an easy shot. If the guard forces him to stop, the dribbler shoots or feeds one of the outside players, who has cut for the basket at an angle of 45 degrees. The cut is started from the point where the foul line, if extended, would strike the sideline.

If it is impossible to get the ball to the middle of the court, the man with the ball continues to dribble on the side, watching always for a man to cut through the middle, perhaps from the opposite side of the court.

Floor balance is of primary importance and it is well to caution players against overcrowding a single area. Floor balance on offense makes for good defensive floor balance if the ball is lost.

Players do not break toward the man with the ball unless he encounters serious trouble. Neither do they move through the middle with the dribbler, since they are only in the way in that sector. It is noteworthy that two players, when too close together, may be guarded adequately by a single defender who knows his business.

Muncie Central teams break in straight lines, because we feel that crisscrossing slows the attack and allows the defense time to form. It is obvious that good ball-handling is essential. Our fast-break slogan is simple but is based on unassailable logic:

LET'S GET THERE AS QUICKLY AS POSSIBLE, BUT LET'S GET THERE WITH THE BALL!

FAST-BREAK PLAYER TYPES

It is quite obvious that players must possess certain mental and physical characteristics to become effective fast-break operators. Front-line players should be big and fast. They should be rugged, willing lads who don't flinch at contact and who are capable of operating with authority in the close work under the basket. They must be able to jump well, start quickly, fake, and dribble. They must be able to pass accurately, because the thrust fails before it is born if the team is unable to get the ball out of the congested area under the goal.

The fast break normally is kept in motion by the guards. These players must be able to take advantage of fast-break situations without delay. They should be the fastest members of the squad and be capable of using the change of pace. They must be able to dribble and pass expertly and hit the basket while moving at top speed.

We call the trailer on the fast-break thrust the "safety valve" of the drive. He is the fourth player who follows a three-man rush. Should the attack bog down, with the middleman unable to pass to either player on the side, he may reverse and pass to the trailer, who often finds an open path to the basket. The trailer may be used in many ways and his duties are explained in diagrams at the end of this chapter.

The fifth man in the fast break moves to the centerline and holds. If his team is forced to slacken and go into its pattern, he takes his normal position. Otherwise, he represents the defense against a quick-forming return thrust and must stay back.

FUNDAMENTAL FAST-BREAK DRILLS

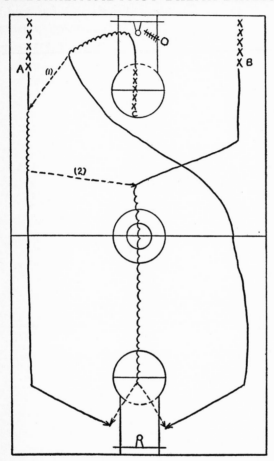

O, *the coach, shoots.* C *rebounds, dribbles, and passes to* A. A *passes to* B, *who has come out to the middle.* C *follows across and behind* B. B *dribbles up the middle. He can keep or pass to* A *or* C.

(Variation 1.) C *passes to* A, *who dribbles to middle of court.* B *goes straight up the floor.* C *fills in in the outside lane to which he has passed.*

(Variation 2.) *To make* C *move, have him rebound, pass to* A, *and then go up the middle to take pass back from* A. B *goes straight up the court.* A *stays on his side;* C *handles the middle.*

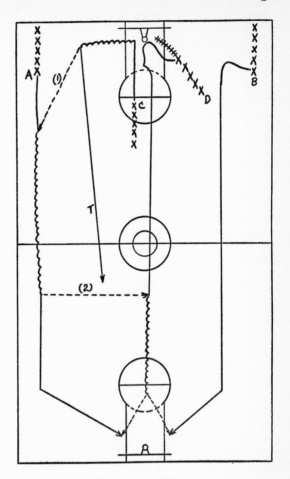

Line D shoots. Line C rebounds, dribbles out, and passes to A. A dribbles and passes to D, the shooter. D dribbles down the middle of court. B fills in in opposite lane. The rebounding line C is the "trailer." Rotation of players is A to B, B to D, D to C, and C to A.

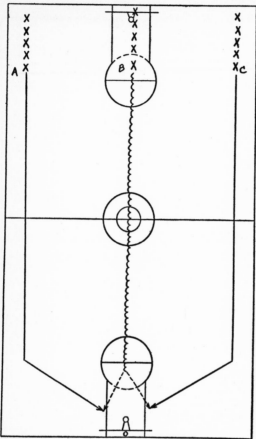

O, *the coach, stands under basket. On the whistle, the first boy in each line advances. The ball is in line* B. *The middle boy dribbles, slows up at outer edge of foul circle. All boys are looking at the coach. The coach, with his hands at his sides, indicates the direction to pass the ball by merely moving his hand on that side. If the coach makes no motion, dribbler drives in for a layup. If the coach holds up both hands, dribbler stops and shoots a jump shot. If the coach holds up both hands and points, the dribbler, even though in the air, feeds off to the cutting man.*

(Variation 1.) *Use bounce and two-hand chest passes.*

(Variation 2.) *Hold up either A or C and then have him catch up.*

(Variation 3.) *Use "trailer" line D. Use signal for middleman to rear turn and hit him.*

FAST-BREAK FORMATIONS

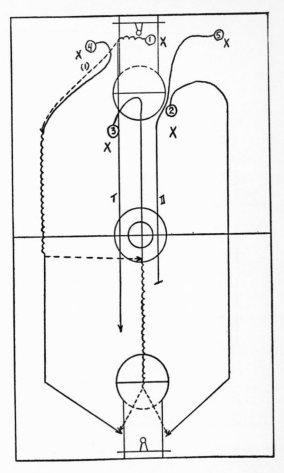

Ball is rebounded by 1, who passes to 4. 4 dribbles and passes to 3,
who dribbles up the middle. 2 fills opposite lane. 1 becomes trailer.
5 becomes defense.

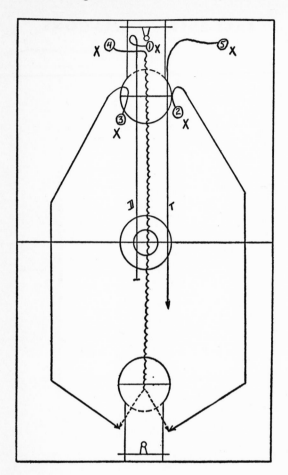

The ball is rebounded by 1, who passes to 4. 3 and 2 fill outside lanes. 4 dribbles up middle. 5 becomes trailer, 1 defense.

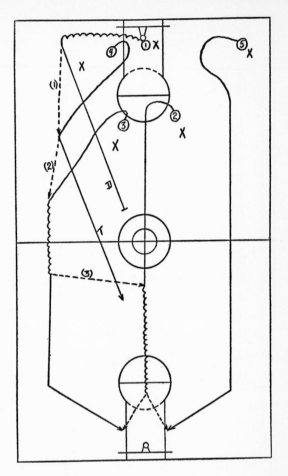

The ball is rebounded by 1, who dribbles out and passes to 4.
4 passes to 3. 2 fills middle lane; 5 fills opposite lane. 3 dribbles
and passes to 2 in middle. 4 becomes trailer, 1 defense.

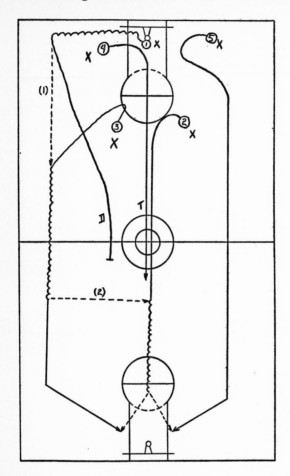

1 *rebounds and passes to 3. 2 fills middle lane. 5 fills opposite lane. 3 dribbles and passes to 2. 4 becomes trailer, 1 defense.*

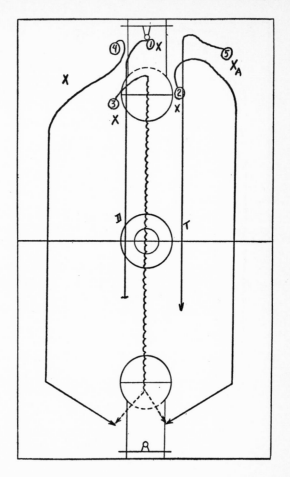

After making a long rebound, 3 turns and dribbles up middle lane.
2 and 4 fill lanes. 1 becomes defense, 5 trailer.

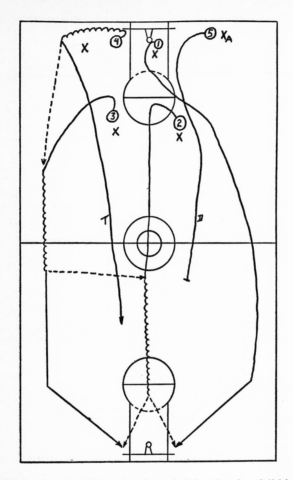

The ball is shot by XA and rebounded by 4, who dribbles and passes to 3. 2 fills middle lane; 1 fills the opposite lane. 3 passes to 2. 4 becomes trailer, 5 defense.

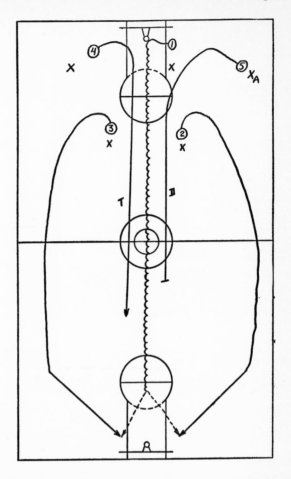

The ball is shot by XA *and rebounded by* 1. 1 *whirls and comes up middle lane.* 2 *and* 3 *fill outside lanes.* 4 *becomes trailer,* 5 *defense.*

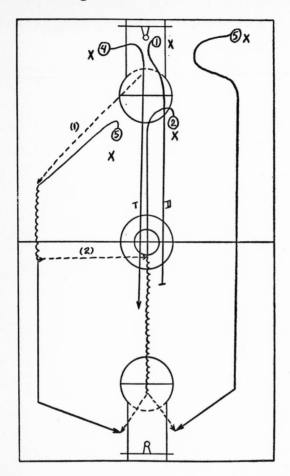

4 makes a semi-long rebound and passes to 3. 2 fills middle lane.
3 passes to 2. 5 fills opposite lane. 4 becomes trailer, 1 defense.

FAST BREAK FROM PASS INTERCEPTIONS

Guard-to-forward pass

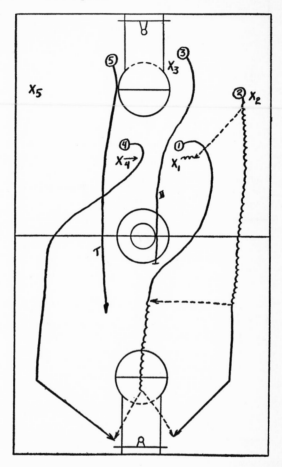

X1 *dribbles and passes toward* X2. *2 intercepts, dribbles, and passes to 1, who takes middle of floor. 1 dribbles up middle. 4 fills side-line lane opposite 2. 5 is trailer; 3 is on defense.*

Guard-to-guard pass

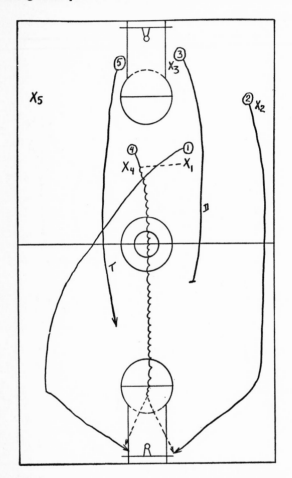

X1 *passes toward* X4. 4 *intercepts and dribbles up middle.* 1 *goes behind* 4 *and fills outside lane.* 2 *fills sideline lane opposite* 1. 5 *is trailer,* 3 *defense. An interception of this type usually affords the interceptor a clear path to the goal.* 1 *follows in case of a missed shot.*

Guard-to-pivot pass

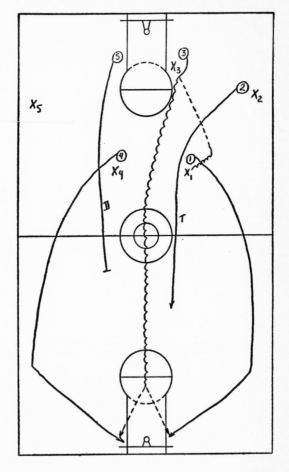

X1 *dribbles and passes toward X3. 3 intercepts and dribbles up the*
middle. 1 and 4 fill respective lanes on their sides of floor. 2 is
trailer, 5 defense.

FAST BREAK FROM MISSED FOUL SHOT

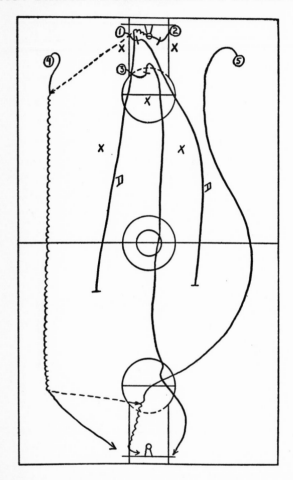

(Option When Ball Cannot Be Passed to Middleman.) *Ball is rebounded by 2, who tips ball to 4. 3 fills middle lane. 5 fills in his own lane. 4 dribbles. 3 continues in middle, then sets block for 5. 5 cuts off 3. 4 passes to 5, who dribbles in. 3 rebounds; 4 rebounds. 1 and 2 are on defense.*

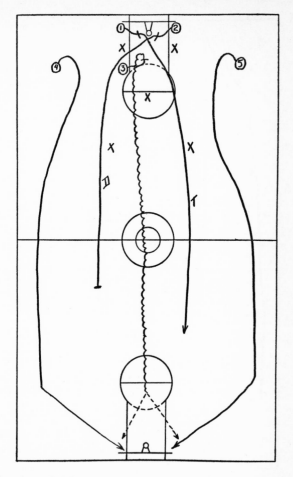

Ball is rebounded by 3, who whirls and dribbles downcourt. 4 and 5 fill lanes on their sides. 1 becomes trailer; 2 is defense safety valve.

(Option.) *3 may pass to 5. 5 dribbles through middle. 3 goes behind 5 and fills lane on side previously occupied by 5. 4 fills his lane. 1 is trailer; 2 is defense safety valve.*

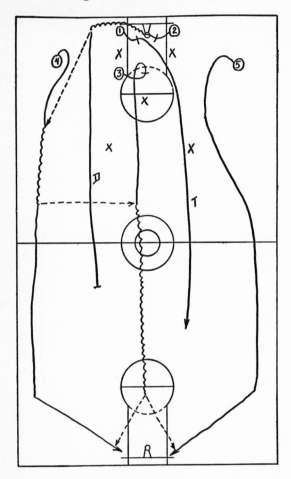

Ball is rebounded by 2. 2 dribbles out and passes to 4. 4 dribbles and passes to 3, who fills middle lane. 3 dribbles as shown. 4 continues in lane on his side. 5 fills lane on opposite side of floor. 1 becomes trailer; 2 is defense safety valve. 3 has option of passing either to 4 or 5. If nobody defenses him, 3 dribbles in.

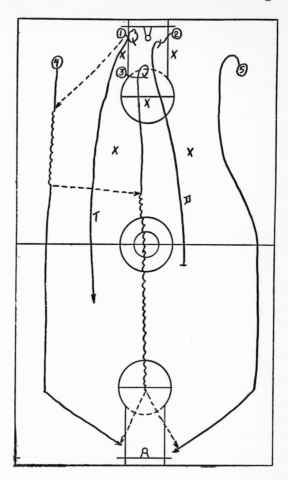

Ball is rebounded by 1 and passed out to 4. 4 dribbles and passes to 3 in middle lane. 4 fills his lane and 5 his lane. 1 is trailer; 2 is defense safety valve.

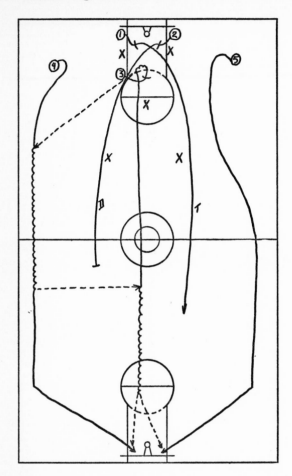

After catching a long rebound, 3 passes to 4 and fills the middle lane. 5 fills his lane. 4 dribbles and passes to 3. 3 dribbles. 1 is trailer; 2 is defense safety valve.

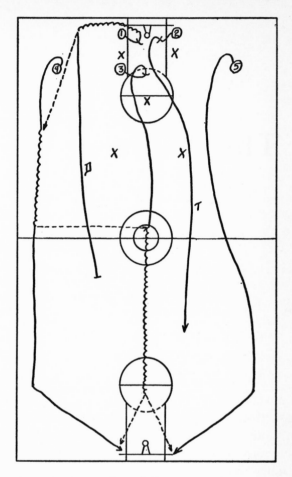

Ball is rebounded by 1, who dribbles toward corner and passes to 4. 4 dribbles and passes to 3 in middle lane. 5 fills his lane. 1 is defense safety valve; 3 trails.

• The defense

THE OFFENSE HAS IMPROVED SO DRAMATICALLY IN MODERN basketball that the defense is hard pressed to remain within shouting distance. The offense today is armed with a greater variety of shots than ever before. The one-hand jump shot cannot be stopped and can be launched from any point on the court. If it is accurate, the opposition has two points; if not, the defense gets another chance, although it is a slim one. Present-day players move faster and more often than their predecessors. Every player is a scoring threat.

Granting that the lot of the defensive player is a grim one, it still is necessary for him to master certain funda-

127

mentals of guarding. These are basic, no matter what type
of team defense is used. Proper stance and well-executed
fundamentals in defense are of vital importance. A team is
no stronger than its weakest defensive player.

INDIVIDUAL DEFENSE

Most coaches agree that balance is without question
the most important single factor in individual defense.
Balance, or stance, usually is divided into two categories,
one of which is called the stride, staggered, or boxer's
stance, the other the parallel stance.

In the stride stance the feet are spread, with one slightly
in front of the other. The distance between the toe of the
rear foot and the heel of the front foot is a matter that
must be determined by the individual. The stance must
be comfortable, yet wide enough for good balance.

The body is held slightly forward with knees flexed and
hips flexed slightly. The back is comparatively straight, the
head is up, and the eyes should be focused on the opponent
at throat level to enable the defensive player to see the
opponent's entire body from feet to head. Arms and hands
help with balance. Some players prefer to hold one hand
high, the other low, although a medium position usually
makes for the best body balance. Technically, the arm on
the side of the front foot should be the higher.

Some coaches insist that the player's feet point straight
ahead. This is good providing the anatomy of the feet will
permit it. Some boys who have what are called "duck feet"
—feet that are naturally held at an angle—find it next to
impossible to point their feet straight ahead. The writer
has found that it is best to permit the player to use the
foot position that is most comfortable to him.

Three-fourths of the weight should be placed on the balls of the feet, the remainder on the heels. If all the weight is on the balls of the feet, the player is under strain and will be forced to use an upward and backward motion when he retreats. Such an unnatural motion often enables the offensive man to go around his defender.

Use of the stride stance. The stride stance is used under the following conditions: (*1*) when defending against a forward on the same side of the floor as the ball, (*2*) when defending against a player who has the ball and has not dribbled, and (*3*) when defending against the pivot man in certain situations. The defender takes a position a little more than arm's length from his opponent. He dogs the man by stabbing at him in an effort to force him to declare himself by means of a dribble or pass. The defender must at all times remain on the floor and does not leap into the air. Should the man with the ball bring the ball to a shooting position, the defender moves close enough to make the shot unnatural. Never permit a player to shoot unmolested. When the player brings the ball down, the defender retreats to his normal position. If he feints, the defender meets all feints with a short step to the side of the fake. If he passes, the defender retreats slightly but strives to remain between his man and the basket. Should the player begin a dribble, the defender changes to a parallel, or "gliding," stance.

Use of the parallel stance. Body position for the parallel stance is similar to that of the boxer's stance except for the position of the feet, which are parallel. This is an excellent stance to guard a man who is dribbling, to guard the pivot man on high post, and to drop away from a man on the weak side.

As the offensive man begins dribbling, the defender adopts a gliding motion with his feet. Using the hand closest to the ball, the defender stabs at the ball with an upward motion of the hand and arm and seeks to force the offensive player away from the effective area. For instance, if a player attempts to dribble to the middle, the defender attempts to force him to the sideline. The defender tries always to keep the offensive man from moving in the direction of the basket.

If the dribbler stops his dribble, the defender swarms over him quickly in an effort to force him to pass hurriedly, often without accuracy. When the pass is made, the defender retreats to a safe distance to make it impossible for the offensive man to circle him and receive a return pass. In meeting a feint, the defender steps in the direction of the feint, using short steps. He generally avoids crossstepping.

TEAM DEFENSE

It is obvious that in any discussion of defense the logical starting point is individual defensive skill. It is just as obvious that the second step is team defense, in which individual skill is utilized.

Many coaches, in this era of net-burning, are convinced that, if their teams are armed with powerful offenses, defense will take care of itself. Such thinking is dangerous because there are nights when the slickest of offenses, for one reason or another, refuses to slip into high gear. What then? The team that is equipped to stop its opponent, or hold him to a moderate total, always has a chance to begin clicking and come on to win. Not so the team that depends solely on its ability to outscore every rival.

At Muncie Central we spend 40 to 50 per cent of our time on defense, individual and team. Each Monday practice is devoted to defense work. Defense gets approximately 20 per cent of the working time Tuesday and Wednesday, and on Thursday, the day before a game, the offense-defense work ratio is about fifty-fifty.

During our season we normally play five weekend double-headers, with games Friday and Saturday nights. But our practice work on defense is limited to that to be used in the Friday game, partly because we do not wish to confuse our players and partly because the Friday night game usually is an important conference game.

Our standard defense is the switching, or shifting man-to-man. It is unlikely that a high school team can learn and use effectively three or four widely varied defenses. For this reason we stick to the man-to-man, switching men when forced to do so and sloughing off the weak side in a semi-collapse.

Team defense actually is the bringing together of five well-trained individual guards. Every guard should be required to learn the defensive requirements for each position. Only in this way is each player able to meet defensive demands when outside his normal territory.

Every player must be able to free-lance on defense, thus avoiding picks or screens and remaining out of trouble while keeping his man under observance. The good defensive man must help a teammate who is in difficulty. In our system, when a dribbler escapes his guard, it becomes the duty of our closest man to pick him up and stall his drive toward the basket. The guard in such a situation stabs at the ball and shouts at his opponent in an effort to confuse him. The other defender is expected to get out of trouble as quickly as possible, pick up the man of the guard who has taken his own man, or re-establish his defensive position against the original player.

"SELLING" THE DEFENSE

Defense must be sold to a team. Players must be shown that it is possible to be a star on defense and that the defensive expert is just as valuable to his team as the man who throws the field goal that wins the game. Defense is a group task, and one player who fails to carry out his defensive assignments hurts his team badly.

There will always be a place for the star defense man. Onlookers in the stands may not be aware of his value, but the coach knows his worth. It is well for the coach to make it plain to his players that he himself is defense conscious and that he does not intend for any player to neglect defensive play while learning the skills of the more glamorous offense. Our players drill constantly on the change from offense to defense. We believe that unless we are able to make the change instantly we give our opponents an advantage.

Coaches occasionally tell their players, "If you must rest, rest on defense." The writer never has cared much for that philosophy, since he sees no particular advantage in working hard for a field goal, then easing to permit an opponent to cancel out those two points with a field goal of his own. Field goals are hard to come by. The time to rest is after the season ends.

The coach must know the defensive abilities of his players in order to fit them into the team defense pattern. There are some players—and may Allah send many more! —who love defense. One Muncie Central player was so proud of his defensive ability that he asked to be assigned to the strongest opposing player in each game. He was given his wish, and each time he carried out his assignment in such a manner that a happy coach often was able to forget completely the chief enemy gunner.

Properly "sold" on the proposition that defense is a worthwhile part of the game, a player becomes a bulldog who is determined to prevent his man not only from scoring, but even from getting the ball! It becomes a personal thing with him—a challenge.

While always alert, the good defense man moves about the court unhampered by fear of blocks or screens. These perils can be met by talking among players, and wise coaches encourage a system of warnings and instructions. The comradely cry, "Pick, Joe!" has headed off many thrusts that would have produced easy baskets. When a warning upsets plans for a pickoff, the man in danger, if he retreats a step and a half, often will discover that the "picker" has returned to his own position, abandoning the pick as no longer feasible. Finger-pointing is another means of team communication on defense. A talking defense is a defense bulwarked by good team spirit and confidence.

SWITCHING MAN-TO-MAN DEFENSE

The switching, or shifting, man-to-man defense, although hardly new, has become more popular during the last decade as the game has speeded up. Constant drilling is necessary for deft, fast operation of the switch from one offensive man to another. Each player must know the defense habits of all his teammates. The player should never assume that a teammate is going to switch, although often a player may anticipate a switch. To be on the safe side, the switch should be called.

When an offensive man shakes his defender it is the duty of the defensive player to whirl immediately and make every effort to get back to his man. As he reverses, the defensive man extends his arms to their full length in an effort to knock down a pass. He watches his opponent's eyes, since it is only natural for a player receiving the ball to follow its flight in the air.

The switching man-to-man defense requires more team play than any other defense. But any defense, to be effective, must be built on cooperation. The switching man-to-man makes it possible to match players to opponents. It aids in pinpointing individual responsibility.

Although a team should be prepared to switch at any time, actual switching situations are not so numerous as might be expected. If the defense against a specific opponent calls for switching each time the guards cross, it should be used only in that situation against that particular opponent.

During the past two years many coaches have found value in switching a guard and forward defensively when the guard passes the ball to the forward and goes outside for his drive. Also, switching is done by guards and forwards when the offensive forward moves out to pick for the offensive guard.

When our scouting reports tell us that opposing guards pass to the pivot and then cross off the pivot, we switch defensively, back up, and cut off the guards' cutting lanes. Each type of switching is shown in diagrams at the end of this chapter.

It is necessary for players to be able to switch on defense when helping one another cover players leading a fast break. One player covers two opponents in this situation, or two players take three offensive men. These defenders steal the ball if possible, but their main function is to slow the attack until help arrives. It is often possible to stall such a drive completely if players are adept at switching while moving fast.

Switching often is necessary to cover a player who is in a favorable position to score and who is not covered by his regular defender. Usually this type of switch is handled by the defensive pivot man, who picks up offensive players who have shaken their defenders.

It is important for both defensive players involved in a switch of opponents to know what is happening. Some coaches permit switching only when players are near enough to touch one another. Switching should not be overdone, since it sometimes causes players to become lazy in carrying out their assignments. Defenders should fight their way through to their men whenever possible. The complaint of some coaches that a switching man-to-man defense tires the defenders is not valid. Proper conditioning is the answer to that one.

The good defensive player never turns his back on his man. Our rule in this situation is, "If you must lose sight of either the ball or your man, lose sight of the ball." We are convinced that the ball isn't going to get into the basket by itself.

No player should relax on defense, even in a game in which there is little real action. The time to relax is during the halftime intermission, or after the game is over.

Player cooperation always is necessary in defensive play. Nearly always our players permit teammates to go through to pick up their men. On the side of the court, after an enemy guard has passed to the forward and has gone outside, our defensive player taking the forward steps back far enough to permit the defensive guard to pass between the two men. When the man is through, the other defender promptly resumes his position on his own man.

SCREENING THE SHOOTER AFTER A FIELD GOAL ATTEMPT

Theoretically, if every player were to screen his man away from the basket properly, the offensive team would obtain no more than 20 per cent of the offensive rebounds. But it doesn't work out that way and many good teams have been killed by that second shot.

This type of screening, then, is a vital part of team defense. When a shot is launched the defensive man screens out the shooter by placing himself between the shooter and the basket. Contact must be avoided and the defender ordinarily may escape contact, and a certain foul, by waiting until his man has chosen a path toward the basket for a possible rebound before stepping in front of him. It is necessary for the defender to watch the offensive man closely, since he may change direction and approach the basket by a different route. Easiest to screen is the pivot man, because the distance to be covered is shorter. The "out" men are more difficult to screen, but it must be done if follow-up baskets are to be avoided.

DEFENSE AGAINST THE PIVOT MAN

Defense against the pivot man may combine a part of the work of two players: the center and the weak-side forward. A part of every practice session should be devoted to work in this particular defense. Pivot defense must be governed by a set of rules to which every member of the team adheres strictly. If the enemy pivot man operates from the baseline to a point halfway to the foul line, play in front of him. Should he move forward into the area between that point and the foul line itself, play at the side of the ball. Should he move beyond the foul line, play behind him, but remain within arm's length when he is in position to take part in an offensive thrust. If he is given the ball, move in close. A boy playing a high post (beyond the foul circle), usually is being used as a feeder. Diagrams at the end of this chapter show the proper positions for defense against the pivot.

When the opposing center is deep and the defensive center is in front of him, it is the duty of the weak-side forward to guard against a high, looping pass. His job is to steal the pass if possible, and if he fails he should take the pivot man defensively. The same rule holds good when defending on the side of the offensive pivot. Any time a player believes he can intercept a pass to the pivot position he is authorized to take the gamble. When he does gamble it is the job of the weak-side forward to cover for him. If necessary, the defender gets help also from the weak-side guard, who drops off in case of emergency.

If the pivot man moves away from the ball—usually to screen the cut of a forward—he should be allowed to go unmolested. But although ignoring him, the defense should make certain that it is in position to pick him up if he doubles back for a pass.

Scouting reports will reveal whether an opponent is a right-handed or a left-handed shooter. Armed with that knowledge, the defense should do everything in its power to force him to shoot from an unnatural or awkward position. If there is one ironclad rule in defense it is this:

NEVER ALLOW AN ENEMY OFFENSIVE PLAYER TO DO THE
THING HE WANTS TO DO.

In the final analysis, defense depends on the opposition. If at least two of the five men who face it are poor ball-handlers or are slow afoot, the defense must operate aggressively in an effort to force them to commit errors that may result in pass interceptions. If they are clever dribblers and deft ball-handlers, the defense must take considerably more caution and tend to float away from the ball. If they are inclined to play the set pattern game, strive to keep them from going into their offensive pattern—usually with a halfcourt press.

THE SLOUGHING AND COLLAPSING DEFENSES

The sloughing defense is a maneuver in which the two players on the side away from the ball—the weak side—drop clear of their opponents to close in around the foul circle. This is diagrammed at the end of this chapter. The sloughing defense is used against a big pivot man and as a means of jamming the middle of the offensive court to prevent a forward from crossing and receiving a pass.

Another method of jamming the middle is the collapsing defense. When this is employed defenders forsake every offensive player except the man with the ball. Diagrams of the collapsing defense also accompany this chapter.

THE HALFCOURT PRESS

A keen-edged tool developed for a specific job—that's the halfcourt press. It is reasonably new in the high school game. The fullcourt press has been recognized as an integral part of modern-day basketball, but high school coaches usually are unable to use it effectively because of lack of squad depth. The halfcourt press is the answer.

The purpose of the halfcourt press is twofold: (1) To keep the offensive team from getting into its pattern or style of play. (2) To put the offensive team on defense—that is, to make the offensive team overcautious in its passing and dribbling. This caution will result in more than the usual number of bad passes, thus giving the defense a greater opportunity for interception.

The Muncie Central team of 1952, a "pony express" outfit that won the Hoosier prep championship, utilized the halfcourt press because it was made up of players who lacked not only height, but weight as well. Each of our fundamental drills in that defense included work on the various phases of the press: namely, footwork, switching or checking when caught in blocks or screens, and overplaying. To accomplish our aims, we worked constantly on one-on-one, two-on-two, and three-on-three drills. Each of the units advanced the ball under simulated game conditions. Usually no more than three players were used on each side in the drilling because we learned that in about 80 per cent of the cases no more than three actually were involved in advancing the ball offensively.

When the halfcourt press is employed it must be kept in mind that a definite type of personnel is needed. Players must be quick, fast, agile, and aggressive. They must have a good sense of timing, the ability to handle the ball while moving at top speed, and, above all, the knack of working as a unit. Probably the most important individuals are the two front men, who press the players advancing the ball. These two players should be the best fundamentally. Their first duty is to stop the players who are bringing the ball downcourt. The three back men must be alert and overplay for interceptions. The defensive man who is guarding the forward opposite the ball practically ignores him. This is diagrammed at the end of this chapter.

THE ZONE DEFENSE

The zone defense is a little like the weather and the common cold. Nobody seems to know what to do about it. It is a powerful force in modern basketball and, as long as it remains a legitimate part of the game, must be studied and understood. The zone defense, in which the ball is guarded rather than the player, has many variations: 2-3, 3-2, 2-2-1, 2-1-2, 1-2-2, 1-3-1, and occasionally an arrangement under which three men are used under the basket, with the two "out" men playing man-to-man. The principal discussion here will involve the 2-3 zone, since this is the most popular. Proper use of the zone defense requires exceptional team unity and understanding. Because it involves almost continuous movement, players must know what they are about if they are to play the ball and still defend their particular areas.

In this day of collapsing defense and weak-side drop-off it is sometimes difficult for the coach to tell whether a true zone actually is being used against him. A simple test usually provides the information he needs. Send a player straight through the middle — if he is completely ignored by his defensive man, you may be reasonably certain that you are facing the zone defense.

When the zone is used each member of the defending team moves as a single unit toward the ball each time it is passed by the offense. Defending players hold arms high or outstretched to knock down passes, which often are thrown recklessly as the defense swarms over the man with the ball. The player closest to the man guards him aggressively to force him to shoot or pass from an unnatural position.

The most important individual in the zone defense is the center. He defends the dangerous offensive area directly in front of the goal, as well as the endline and short corners. While this is admittedly a large order, the center is given aid by the weak-side forward and guard when he leaves his original position. The forward moves in front of the basket and the guard defends the outer edge of the foul circle. Both are alert for a cut from the weak side.

A team whose members are only fairly mobile may use the zone to good advantage, especially if it includes three tall men. These players normally are in good position to rebound. The zone usually neutralizes blocks and screens used by the offensive team and is especially effective if the offensive team shoots poorly from outside.

Players foul less when using the zone, a tremendous factor in this day of close officiating and severe penalties for fouling. Fouling is reduced to a minimum largely because defenders are responsible for smaller areas and usually are not required to fight their way through screens and blocks.

The zone defense makes it difficult for the opponent to obtain short shots and affords many opportunities for pass interceptions. Players are in position to gamble for interceptions, since they are secure in the knowledge that a teammate is backing their play. The zone is less difficult to coach than the man-to-man because of the smaller number of defensive situations arising.

Like all other defenses, the zone has its faults. It is not effective against a fast-breaking team and fails miserably if the opponent is equipped with deadly outside shooters. It is often ineffective against a delayed attack and it sometimes allows the attacking team to throw two players into an area defended by only one player.

Despite these flaws, the zone defense is a formidable proposition when correctly used. It is particularly effective against the team that uses careful pattern work, coupled with a good blocking game, to break players loose for good shots. The defense is diagrammed on the following pages.

TEAM DEFENSE

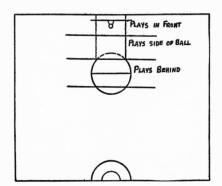

(Left.) *Defense against the pivot.*

(Right.) *1 and 2 play tight. 3 is loose for possible interception. 4 is fairly tight. 5 drops to foul line to cover lob pass to X3. 5 will defense X3 if he gets away from 3. This is the basic defensive team position. If ball is on opposite side of court, defense changes to that side in same manner.*

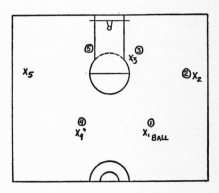

(Right.) *Here is defensive movement if* X1 *passes to* X2 *and cuts.* 2 *steps back to allow* 1 *to go through.* 1 *keeps a hand up while going through to keep* X2 *from shooting. When* 1 *calls, "Through,"* 2 *resumes tight position on* X2. *Notice movement of* 4, *whose actions are determined by movements of* X4.

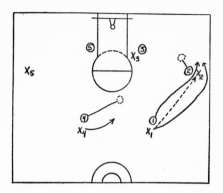

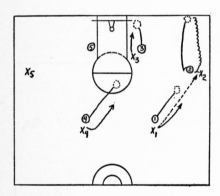

(Left.) *If* X2 *fakes and drives to endline, losing* 2, 2 *makes every effort to pick him up as shown. In next diagrams, movements are shown if switch is necessary. Note movements of* 1 *and* 4 *above.*

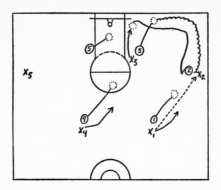

(Left.) *If X2 gets away from 2 and 2 cannot cover him successfully, we switch. 2 takes X3 and 3 takes X2. Note 5 dropping to help on X3. Also note position of 4.*

(Right.) X2 *moves out to block for X1. 2 warns 1 and 1 backs up. 2 plays loose. If block is not successful, there is no switch. If X1 gets past block, 2 switches to X1. 1 takes X2.*

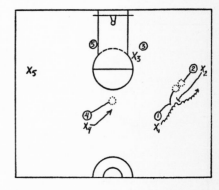

(Right.) *Defensive pattern if forwards and center play deep. Also defensive movement if X2 and X3 both come out. Note pick-up by 2. 3 overplays. If X2 gets ball, 3 assumes standard defense of pivot. 5 holds.*

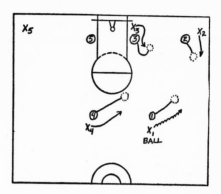

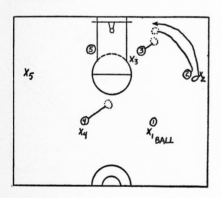

(Left.) *If X2 comes out, whirls, and expects lead pass from X1, 2 whirls with him and throws arms high in effort to block pass. 3, alert to what is happening, is ready for possible interception. If pass is thrown, 4 retreats. 5 holds.*

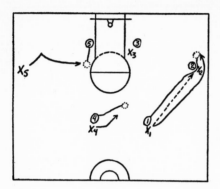

(Left.) *Scouting reports show that X5 comes across middle. Notice movements of 5. As X5 moves, 5 moves to head him off. 5 keeps outside arm in front of X5.*

(Right.) X3 *goes away from ball.* X5 *comes across middle.* 5 *moves out to cut off* X5. 3 *takes defense position in front of* X3, *as shown.*

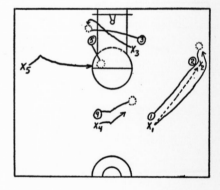

(Right.) *If pass goes to X3, 3 gets behind. 2 drops off to help if possible, but watches X2. If X3 goes to his right, 5 helps out. 1 retreats one and one-half steps to keep position on X1. 4 drops back. 5 holds.*

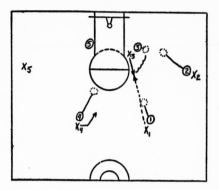

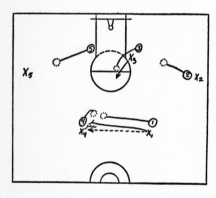

(Left.) *X1 passes to X4 and sets block. If X4 takes advantage and is successful, 1 switches to X4 and and 4 takes X1. We try to catch X4 in his first dribble. Occasionally 1 and 4 play aggressively against man with ball and ignore X1. 5 moves out because ball is on his side of floor. 2 drops off. 3 plays standard position.*

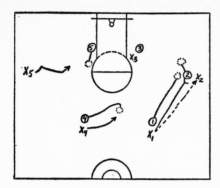

(Left.) *Inside pick by* X1 *on* 2 *after passing to* X2. 2 *steps back one step and is more concerned with side- and endlines. If* X2 *uses block to advantage, 1 and 2 switch. 1 takes* X2 *and 2 takes* X1. *Movements of 4 and 5 are determined by* X4 *and* X5. *If* X2 *prefers sideline to endline, there is no switch between 1 and 2.*

(Right.) X1 *passes to* X3 *and cuts.* X4 *cuts off* X1. 1 *and 4 switch: 1 takes* X4 *and 4 takes* X1. 2 *plays less tightly. 5 already is in position. 3 follows standard rule of pivot defense.*

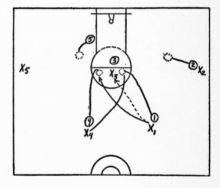

(Right.) X1 *passes to X2.*
X3 comes to same side as
ball. X2 *passes to X3 and*
cuts. No switches. 1, 4,
and 5 *slough off as dia-*
grammed.

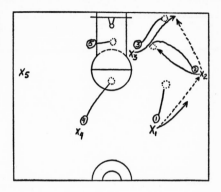

THE HALFCOURT PRESS

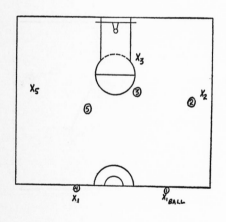

(Left.) 4 *and* 1 *start the*
press three to five feet over
the centerline. 2, 3, *and* 5
overplay their men for in-
terceptions. Note position
of 5 *in relation to ball.* 3
plays his man loosely.

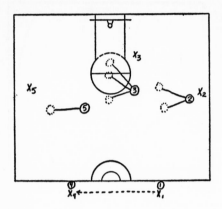

(Left.) *Defensive position when ball is passed from X1 to X4. 4 and 1 press constantly. Movements of 2, 3, and 5 depend primarily on movements of X2, X3, and X5; and they continue to overplay.*

(Right.) *An attempted interception by 4 when the ball is passed from X1 to X4. Note the interchange of 1 and 4 if the attempt fails. 1 takes X4 and 4 takes X1. The probable movement of the offense and defense, if the interception fails, is also shown.*

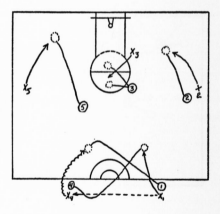

(Right.) *An attempted interception by 2 when the ball is passed from X1 to X2. Note the interchange, defensively, between 2 and 3. 2 takes X3 and 3 takes X2. Diagram also shows the probable movement of the offense and defense if the interception fails.*

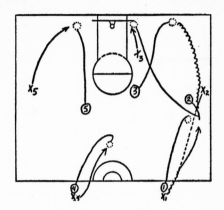

THE ZONE DEFENSE

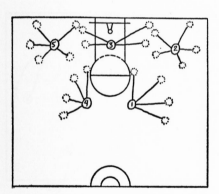

(Left.) *Usual floor position of the 2-3 zone, with approximate areas of coverage. However, if the ball is in a particular zone, the defensive player plays the ball aggressively.*

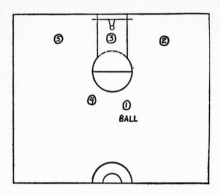

(Left.) *This and the following diagrams show zone positions relative to the ball as it is dribbled or passed.*

(Right.) *Ball starts to sideline.*

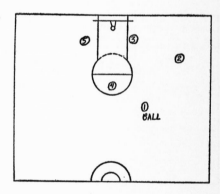

(Right.) *Ball on side of court. Possibility of a double-team on B by 1 and 2.*

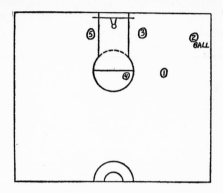

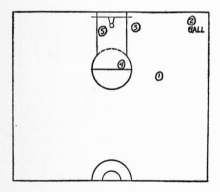

(Left.) *Ball in corner.*

SLOUGHING DEFENSE

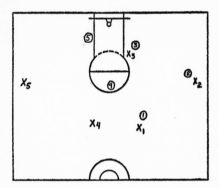

(Left.) *Team defensive positions as ball is passed by* X1 *to* X2.

COLLAPSING DEFENSE

(Right.) *Team defensive positions as ball is passed from* X1 *to* X2. *Note position of* 1 *after ball is passed.*

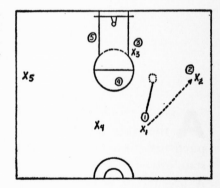

• Preparing for
the tournament

ALONG ABOUT HALF-PAST FEBRUARY IN MOST STATES,
they take the bedraggled old basketball coach and
pitch him into the pressure cooker. In other words, the
state interscholastic basketball tournament gets underway.
A breeder of untold mental anguish, a bomb that has
been known to blow the jobs of coaches right out from
under them, the state tourney nevertheless has its ad-
vantages. For the coach whose season has been a dismal
one, it offers salvation in the form of an upset victory. For

155

many teams the season is a complete success if a tried and true enemy is ambushed somewhere along the tourney trail. Often it doesn't make much difference what happens in the next game. And there are always those championships, which are lovely from any angle.

The tournament has a way of sneaking up on the coach, who often wonders what happened to his season. There just weren't enough hours in enough days. The coach who nears tourney eve with preparation still ahead of him is a dead one, and will learn it early. Tournament preparation cannot be accomplished in a week or a month. It is a season-long process of conditioning, of polishing offense and defense, and of little lessons in psychology.

To be sure, late-season injuries or illness may wreck the plans of the most careful coach, and he has no way of knowing exactly what will be thrown at him by each opponent. But certain things can be done to ready a team gradually for its tournament effort, and the smart coach does them.

Vaccine, administered during the season, helps head off the flu. Vitamins keep young players fit and eager, even though they are finely drawn. Questionable ankles may be protected through the season by careful taping.

If offensive and defensive patterns have been designed to work against any enemy, there is no need for coach or players to fret about surprise tactics. It isn't likely that any coach will change his style completely within a week or two in order to overturn a favorite foe in a tournament. Such jerry-built offenses fall apart more often than they hold together. Our Muncie Central teams take their normal offensive and defensive patterns into the year-end tournament. Through the season we seek to build up our reserve strength to guard against weariness in the grueling tournament schedule—a schedule that often requires a team to play as many as four games in a single weekend. Two tourney games in a single day are the rule rather than the exception in Indiana, although no team is permitted to play more than twice in a twenty-four hour span.

Naturally, a team should expect to be in top physical condition when a tournament arrives late in February. Proper conditioning is the most important single factor in tourney preparation. The tired team doesn't react quickly, or shoot well.

If there are *four* days between the last regularly scheduled game and the first tourney game, the practice routine need not be changed. If there are *three* days, the Monday and Tuesday practices may be the same, and then on Wednesday the team can run briskly through offensive and defensive patterns, shoot fouls briefly, and head for the shower room.

The coach's *first* concern is with the *first* tourney opponent: Play them one at a time. The first opponent is the greatest of them all. Then, if he is beaten, the next opponent is the target of targets. Never jump over a supposedly weak opponent to concentrate on a strong foeman. Teams that forget weak opponents often don't get to play the strong one for which they pointed.

● Scouting
the opponent

THE MODERN-DAY BASKETBALL SCOUT, UNLIKE HIS predecessor, walks in as if he owned the place. There was a time when this seeker after knowledge bought his own ticket furtively, crept into the arena with coat-collar turned up and hatbrim down, and set up operations in its darkest corner. Now coaches see the same scouts so often that they confuse them with members of their own staffs. The modern scout picks up free tickets at the box-office, breezes into the gym with a roll of blank paper under his arm, inquires after the health of the doorman's mother-in-law, whom he knows personally, and installs himself in the pressbox or one of the better reserved-seat sections. Pretty girls often fetch him cold drinks—on the house!

Good scouting is an important part of basketball. It helps win games and is a completely serious business to the serious coach. Tools of the careful scout include a clipboard in case no table is available, blank floor diagrams, shot charts, plenty of pencils, and the knack of concentrating on a reasonably complicated job.

The good scout plans his schedule for the season well in advance and gives ticket managers ample time to arrange for his visit. Notice of at least a week not only insures a good seat but is a courteous gesture. A seat as high as possible above the floor makes his task easier.

It is well to arrive before the varsity team reaches the court. The reserve team usually employs the same offensive pattern and it is necessary in any case to watch varsity players during their pregame warmup. Does a certain player shoot always from the same side of the floor? Does the pivot man practice only hooks, or does he shoot occasionally from outside?

A program is of course a necessity, and the scout can only hope that the coach who made up the program roster is a God-fearing fellow who never fails to present a true picture of the height and weight of his athletes. The number of letters won and uniform numbers are bits of information that may be gleaned from the program.

After writing the names and numbers of starters on his first sheet, the scout thereafter uses only uniform numbers in his charts. The position of each player prior to the opening tipoff is noted, as are individual positions on offense and defense. When a substitute enters the game his number is placed beside that of the player he replaced. A circle around his number pegs him as a reserve. His time of entry is noted.

The team's general offensive pattern is identified. Is it free-lance, control, semi-control, pivot play? All options are charted as they unfold, as are out-of-bounds plays and methods of advancing the ball. Does the team fast break? If the answer is yes, where does the first pass go? What type of fast break is used? Are the passes generally short, medium length, or long? Is the dribble used extensively? Who leads the break in most cases? What lanes do players prefer? How can this particular fast break be halted? Is the team usually in position to get back on defense if an error costs possession? Is the rush a two-, three-, or four-man affair?

As for other offense, the scout asks himself these questions: Does the team follow a set pattern? Who are the key players? Who makes the team go? How effective are screens and blocks? Will our players be able to get through, or will we have to switch? Are passes short and sharp or will it be possible for us to intercept? Has the team any "pet" plays that are used at specific times, such as after a time-out or at the beginning of a period? How strong is this team on the offensive board? Who is the best rebounder? Who are the best shooters? Is there an offensive weakness? Does the team like to run, or does it avoid the running game? Does it ever change its general tactics after the game has started? Is there a defensive weakness? Who is the weakest defensive player? Who is the strongest? What is the physical condition of this team?

Individually: How does each player shoot? Is he right handed, or left? One hand, or two? Who are the drivers? Does an individual player take only good shots? How fast is he? How quickly does he get into his position? Can he fake and drive, give and go? Is he a team player or an individualist? Does he seem sure of himself when he gets the ball? Does he go after loose balls? Which way does he go after passing off or cutting? Which way does he go when he dribbles? What does he do after passing?

Ordinarily, coaches do not often change their general styles through the years, but it is necessary each season to scout new personnel. The careful coach keeps a card index on the players of his opponents, adding a card when a player makes the varsity team and destroying it when he is graduated. It is good practice to scout the same team as often as possible. One visit may pay skimpy rewards if the team happens to play a bad game that night. Opposition strength must be considered. It is sometimes advisable to scout a team as many as eight times in a single season.

The scout who can do so is well advised to take along a helper, who will prove invaluable in charting shots and for other chores. Our scouts chart every shot by number, circling those that produce baskets and identifying them with symbols—*2H* for a two-hand shot, *LU* for layup, etc.

It is well to talk over the game with the helper on the way home, while action is fresh in the minds of both viewers. The scout visualizes defensive alignment and offensive patterns to be used when his own team meets the team he has just seen. Notes are best copied as promptly as possible to avoid loss of detail.

Scouting, properly done, is exacting work and requires close attention. But it pays off in victories. The coach who boasts that he never scouts an opponent is a foolish man— or a lazy one.

• Prevention and treatment of injuries

Some Martian archeologist, poking through the dust-choked ruin of a stateside burying ground in the 30th Century, may scratch one of his pointed little heads in wonderment on brushing the dirt from a headstone that reads, "Here lies good old Coach Doakes—worried to death by a bad knee." The visiting scientist will have no way of knowing that it was somebody else's knee.

Among the occupational hazards of coaching, few are so pestiferous as the common injury. Athletes, being for the most part lean and angular and drawn to a fine edge, are bedeviled constantly by miseries ranging from hangnails to fractures, from Charley horses to churning stomachs. Injuries are more than a nuisance. They have been known to stop winning teams squarely in their tracks. Teams thus stopped sometimes don't get started again. A working knowledge of injuries—their prevention, if possible, and their treatment—is a vital part of the equipment of a coach, since most athletes, sometime, are going to jerk something loose.

All schools should make certain that at least one doctor is available to handle serious athletic injuries, whether they are suffered during actual games or in practice. There are minor injuries, however, that every coach should be able to treat, at least until the athlete is placed in the physician's care. Certainly a doctor should be consulted in all cases in which doubt exists, and his recommendations should be followed to the letter, no matter how much line-up-juggling is necessary. A healthy substitute is far more effective than a banged-up regular. That's why we have substitutes! Here again the coach should bear in mind that his athletes are his personal responsibility and that they will need those knees and arms and ankles long after their basketball equipment has been laid aside. By the same token, no reputable coach would resort to giving a boy medication that would make it possible for him to play when he should not be playing. High school basketball isn't *that* important.

A number of guides are available to the coach and should be in his library. They include Rollie Bevan's *The Athletic Trainer's Handbook,* published, 1955, by Prentice-Hall, Inc., Englewood Cliffs, N. J.; *Helpful Hints from the First-Aider,* published by the Cramer Chemical Company, Gardner, Kansas; *The Trainer's Bible,* by S. E. Belik, M.D., published by T. J. Reed and Company, New York; and the handbook issued by the Bike-Web Company, Chicago, Illinois.

Many schools find it possible to borrow the services of the trainer of a nearby college or university. The writer has found that nearly all of these are willing to share their great knowledge of taping and injury prevention and treatment.

Most colleges now offer, in conjunction with their coaching courses, a course in the care and treatment of athletic injuries. Every prospective coach should enroll if such a course is available. He will bless the day he signed the card.

TREATMENT OF COMMON ATHLETIC INJURIES

Ankle sprains. To treat a sprained ankle the shoe and sock should be removed immediately and the ankle wrapped tightly with the Louisiana wrap, using an Ace bandage. The ankle should be immersed in ice water for twenty minutes, after which the ankle wrap should be removed, the hair shaved from the ankle, and tincture of benzoin applied. After the ankle has dried taping should begin—the basket-weave method is the most effective. An opening should be left at the top to permit swelling. Should the sprain appear to be severe, a physician should be consulted. If there is no swelling or only moderate swelling the following day, the ankle should be soaked in warm salt water.

Most sprains are minor, and for this reason we seldom remove a player completely from practice. Usually he shoots baskets and practices foul shooting and is slowly returned to the normal practice routine. However, if the examining physician indicates that the player should be withheld from practice, this is done immediately, although he is asked to attend practice in street clothes. In this way he feels that he still is a part of the team and shares in team plans.

Continue the soaking treatment until the player is able to operate at full speed. When the tape is removed use an Ace bandage, a protective wrap that is usually worn through the remainder of the season to guard against recurrence of the injury.

Jammed fingers. Jammed fingers are among the most common injuries in athletics. Even though the first impulse of coach or player may be to give the jammed finger a sudden yank, this should not be done. Instead, the finger should be soaked in warm salt water, then anchored to an adjacent finger with two small strips of tape. One strip a fourth of an inch wide should be placed behind the second joint of each finger and another between the first and second joints of the finger. The taping should not be extremely tight. It should permit free movement while protecting the injured finger.

Cuts near the eyes. Here is another common type of injury, and most basketball players have been startled, at some time or another, by a sudden spurt of blood from an eye cut following a collision. These injuries usually are far less serious than they appear. Bleeding may be halted by the application of cold cloths to the area. Ice packs work well also. When bleeding has stopped the area should be sponged with alcohol or any good antiseptic. If stitching is required, that of course is the responsibility of the doctor. But if the cut is not too wide or deep a gauze pad may be taped in place. A new dressing should be applied each day. Eye cuts usually are accompanied by little pain and are dangerous only if they affect the eye itself or are permitted to become infected.

Other small facial lacerations may be treated during

game or practice by washing with alcohol and painting with collodion.

Charley horses. A Charley horse results from a blow to a muscle, which in turn strikes the bone underneath. This contact causes a bruise, which may affect the blood vessels. If the blow is hard enough, the blood vessels may bleed, thus causing a hematoma. This formation is painful and may limit the action of the injured player.

When a player gets a Charley horse, he should be asked to continue exercising, even though it may be painful for him. Apply an ice pack or cold water to limit bleeding; follow up by applying heat. It is best not to massage the injury. To apply constant or prolonged heat, use analgesic packs. Protect the area until the injury is healed. The most common areas for Charley horses are the front part of the thigh and the calf of the leg.

TREATMENT OF COMMON AILMENTS

Blisters and callouses. A basketball team is no better than its feet. A boy whose feet are blistered or calloused operates under a painful handicap. Every precaution should be taken to guard against such conditions. Some boys are seldom bothered by foot blisters, but a great many belong in the tenderfoot class and must be handled accordingly.

At the start of the season each Muncie Central player paints the soles of his feet daily with tincture of benzoin as a toughening precaution. Just as important, we make certain that shoes fit properly. Our players wear an inner sock that is padded at the bottom. The outer sock is of good-quality wool. A generous amount of foot powder is used in each shoe. If a blister appears we first paint the area with Merthiolate. Using a needle that has been dipped in antiseptic solution, we puncture the blister at its base and drain it. Using a cue tip, which is a bit of cotton fastened to the end of a small stick, we paint the blister inside and out with Merthiolate. The area then is padded with gauze or sponge rubber and the boy continues to play.

If a blister appears under a callous, we ask a foot doctor to remove the callous, then treat the blister as outlined above. The treatment of a simple callous is an easy operation. The foot should be soaked in a sodium bicarbonate solution for ten to fifteen minutes to soften the callous. Then use a bunion file to remove as much of the callous as possible.

Floor burns. Floor burns occur when the outer layer of skin has been peeled off by contact with the floor. The area should be washed with soap and water and painted with tincture of benzoin. A careful check should be made to guard against infection.

Ingrown toe nails. Short shoes and improper nail clipping are the chief causes of ingrown toe nails. The area may become inflamed and swollen. Pain often follows. The boy should soak his foot in a sodium bicarbonate solution to soften the nail. The nail is then lifted, and a thin piece of rolled cotton, soaked with Merthiolate, is placed under the nail, thus affording the nail a chance to grow properly. If toe nails are trimmed straight across, they seldom become ingrown.

BAD KNEES—CALL THE DOCTOR!

Readers will note that no effort has been made to describe treatment of that most disastrous of all basketball injuries, the trick knee. The human knee joint is an involved mechanism that, when out of whack, requires the skill of a competent physician. Aside from applying his knowledge of taping—a knowledge, incidentally, that tells him when *not* to tape—the coach usually can do little for these painful and frustrating injuries. If the doctor orders a certain type of protective device, the coach can insist that the player wear it. But essentially the treatment of knee injuries belongs in more practiced hands.

Should the coach desire to squeeze a rabbit's foot or hide his eyes when a star player with a trick knee makes a sudden stop or turn, then by all means he should do so. But mainly it's a job for the doctor.

THE MEDICINE CHEST

Every coach should have at his disposal a number of common items to be used in the prevention and treatment of injuries. Amounts will be determined by the size of the squad. Here are the essentials:

Adhesive tape	Gauze bandages
Alcohol	Merthiolate
Analgesic balm	Powdered rosin
Ankle wraps	Safety razor
Aspirin	Scissors
Band-aids	Smelling salts
Cotton cue tips	Tape remover
Eye-wash	Tongue depressors
Firm-Grip	Tuf-Skin
Foot and body powder	Wood applicators
Foot ointment	

eleven

• Equipping the team

GOOD EQUIPMENT IS WITHIN THE REACH OF EVERY HIGH school, no matter how limited its athletic budget. Since coaches are responsible for buying most equipment, it is necessary for them to know the subject. A little study will make the coach a wise buyer, although most sporting goods houses offer equipment that is sturdy and attractive at reasonable prices.

If a team hopes to be a champion its players should look and feel like champions, in addition to acting like champions. Good taste should be shown in uniform color combinations. High school boys don't feel as if they are bigtimers if their uniforms are smalltime, and there is no reason for a smalltime appearance.

Good shoes are a must, of course, and uniforms should be of good quality as well as attractive. Penny-pinching in the purchase of athletic equipment is definitely unwise. Athletic equipment gets hard use. A team should have as many changes of uniform and warmup equipment as its athletic budget permits, but two sets of good uniforms are a better investment than four sets of shoddy ones.

Players should be proud of their equipment, just as they are proud of their coach, their home community, and their school. Although no coach should take part in a clothing race with other coaches, he should bear in mind that his team is just as "big," just as good, as it looks and feels.

Good basketball equipment must be regarded as part of the cost of doing business. Though it is often possible to cut corners, it is never wise to sacrifice team morale to save dollars. This is especially true when a team is drawing well and the financial picture is bright. High school athletes get no financial rewards. Certainly they are entitled to good equipment.

THE LOCKER ROOM

If there is one place in which the coach and his players are completely together—and shut off from outsiders—it is in the locker room. Here players are given pregame instruction. Here they gather for between-halves encouragement and criticism. They troop back to the locker room when the game is over and the battle won or lost.

This being the case, it is obvious that no locker room should be a dingy hole in the wall. A school need not be rich from the standpoint of athletics to offer its players a bright, cheerful dressing room. The wise coach, sitting with his players in a comfortably arranged locker room, can do much to ease the unbearable tension that often assails young athletes before a game. Personal problems often are worked out in this friendly retreat. If a boy is to be reprimanded it is often best for this to be done privately, rather than before his teammates. It is in the locker room that the team often learns from scouts the ability of its next opponent. Here, shut off from the orations of curbstone coaches, players are exposed to the philosophy of the real coach, the real leader, the man they trust and admire.

The cheers of the crowd, the boos of the fair-weather friends, are far away. The locker room is an important workshop—and a refuge for weary young men who often are emotionally upset. It goes without saying that the locker room should be a friendly place, a clean, wholesome retreat that is as much like home as coach and school can make it.

THE TEAM MANAGER

Nearly all high school teams have student managers. Some are a blessing, some a nuisance. The wise coach will quickly eliminate boys falling into the second category. A well-trained, gentlemanly student manager is a rare jewel.

A good student manager is "Johnny-on-the-spot." He is capable of getting along with all members of the squad, and with boys of varied personalities gathered on a single team—this is often difficult. He is intelligent enough to study the coach and learn to anticipate his wishes. He is the coach's left hand.

He must love the game as much as the boys who are actually playing. He should be physically capable of doing an exacting and arduous job.

The good manager, without having to be told, should pack equipment bags, keep balls pumped up, and be able to keep score and chart shots to the satisfaction of the coach. He often knows more basketball than any player, since he must be familiar with all phases of the game and does not specialize. He should be able to referee scrimmage sessions.

Every school has boys who are vitally interested in basketball but who aren't quite good enough to be varsity players. These are the lads who make the best student managers. It isn't a job for a lazy lad. The good student manager is first at practice and often last to leave. With the managerial details in good hands, the coach is free to concentrate on the other problems of his profession. Certainly there are plenty of these!

THE EQUIPMENT MANAGER

In charge of the student manager at most schools is the equipment manager, and fortunate indeed is the coach who has one. Among his numberless duties, he makes certain that the team has the proper equipment for practice and games. He is responsible for laundry and dry cleaning. He pays officials and handles contract obligations with other schools. He plans trips, orders meals, keeps shot charts, figures percentages, and issues equipment. When the team is on the road he is the traveling secretary.

When it is time to throw out a new ball for a home game the equipment manager has it ready. When the game is over officials find towels laid out in their dressing quarters. The coach himself might like to drown some of them under the shower, but the equipment manager makes them comfortable no matter what the score. He is an example for young athletes: he exults quietly when the team wins and suffers in silence when it loses. A coach who can find among the faculty members of his school a man sufficiently loyal and interested to serve as equipment manager should enlist his aid.

t
w
e
l
v
e

● The winning spirit

WHEN MUNCIE CENTRAL WON THE INDIANA HIGH SCHOOL basketball championship for the second successive year in 1952, a throng of more than 15,000 well-wishers waited long past midnight to welcome us home from Indianapolis. Muncie is a community of barely 60,000 and estimates placed one Muncie resident in four around a huge bonfire at our Fieldhouse. When we lost to Milan in the final game of the 1954 tournament, our unofficial welcoming committee was just as large. In victory and defeat, Muncie was solidly behind us.

Admittedly this may be an extreme example of community support. But the writer believes that every school can and should build up a following and hold that following. Good school and community spirit can be developed in communities where it does not exist; and the school, by the actions of its athletes, coaches, and students, can build respect that produces and retains support even in defeat. In fact, solid support often turns defeat into victory. Every coach knows that high school and college athletes, even professionals, often rise up to win important games because their followers want badly for them to win. Good cheering, directed by good cheer-leaders, is of great value. Game-winning rallies often start in the stands. As for school pep chapels, they have sent second-rate basketball teams roaring into battle with the psychological ammunition to shoot down far stronger foemen.

THE SCHEDULE

A schedule can make or break a high school team and the coach who directs it. It is possible for a coach to compile a gaudy won-lost record. Any coach can do it. All he has to do is find teams weaker than his own—and play them! He may lose occasionally, if he has guessed wrong on some poor assortment that played better than it knew how, but he won't lose many.

But that kind of won-lost record doesn't mean much because it doesn't fool the people who count—school patrons, students, the press. Coaching prestige isn't built on the carcasses of rinky-dinks, and certainly little personal satisfaction is derived from pushing over a pushover.

The coach who intends to move up the success ladder must play good opponents. But he must exercise keen judgment in building a schedule. Too much schedule strength is even more disastrous to team, school, and community morale than too little. Nobody likes to be licked every Friday night and it is easy for the too-ambitious coach to overschedule his team in an effort to add to his personal glory.

Every team should stay in its own league, although occasional excursions into better company are to be desired as prestige-builders for team and coach because every coach should be striving to lift his team into a higher class of competition. A team will have enough to do beating its own kind. And, if it can be brought up to a victory over a so-called "bigger" team, it has only been given a little bonus by the fates that control high school basketball.

A schedule that is too strong kills the desire of any team. A weak schedule destroys its incentive and makes it overconfident. It is the task of the wise coach to find that happy medium, that desirable balance of opponents that will force his team to play businesslike basketball throughout the season.

High school players will tackle any foeman for a coach they respect and love. But they have a right to expect that he will not send them into a sausage grinder. If the team shows gradual improvement through the years of a coach's tenure, then a gradual strengthening of the schedule is in order. But the coach must remember that all schedules should be based on material—the material in prospect in the future. The man who coaches in a small school is especially vulnerable to talent famines. Perhaps his material is of good quality for a few years and he feels capable of moving into stronger competition. But what will happen in five years, when the material isn't there?

The answer, of course, is a succession of whackings and a hasty retreat from the bigtime. This is a humiliating experience that can be avoided if the coach stirs in common sense as the main ingredient of his schedule-making.

A GUEST IN THE HOUSE

A team must be especially careful in its relationships with other schools, bearing in mind always that its players, when they perform in another city, serve as representatives of their hometown. Their role is as ambassadors of good will, no matter what appears on the scoreboard at the close of the game.

A visiting team should accept without complaint what it gets in the way of dressing facilities. No player should tamper with property that is not his own. Players should be encouraged to make friends with their opponents, before the game, if possible. And, although there is nothing better than to win, they should always strive to be gentlemanly losers.

Just as important is the squad's role as host team. At Muncie we strive to treat visiting teams and spectators as if they were guests in our own homes. Players are assigned dressing rooms as good as our own. We reserve a block of tickets for visiting patrons, even though it is necessary to turn away hometown customers to make this possible. Our band plays the school song of the opponent; cheers are exchanged.

When it is possible, we arrange to eat with members of the opposing team after the game. This makes for a feeling of comradeship among players and coaches and usually makes firm friends of lads who were battling bitterly an hour earlier.

THE WINNING HABIT

Nothing succeeds like success. One of the most important factors in a successful high school athletic program is the development of the winning habit.

Oddly, when a school starts winning in one sport, it often wins in all sports. This is due partly to the fact that players of the winning school are given a psychological boost and partly to the fact that opponents often are beaten before they start because they just don't think they are good enough. The team that is confident of winning has a tremendous advantage over the team that isn't quite sure.

The mystic quality called "class" enters into the picture also. Those who are close to high school sports know that teams from small schools don't often beat teams from big schools. By "big" we mean big in the sense of being consistent winners, bigtimers. There are exceptions, of course. Milan, a little team from a little school, won the Indiana high school basketball championship in 1954, beating in the final game, incidentally, Muncie Central.

When a school rides the crest of victory the breaks seem to come its way. But a word of warning: when a team loses that "Indian sign" on its opponents, they hit back hard. Years of labor are necessary to push a school to the top in high school athletics. But a few defeats can take away that intangible advantage, and the road back is a long one. A school makes the climb slowly, but it can leave the bigtime like Steve Brodie left the Brooklyn Bridge.

We want our players to feel a fierce pride in the uniforms they wear. In 1955, after we had lost a one-point tournament game to the Indianapolis Attucks team that was to win the Hoosier prep championship a week later, the writer walked into the Muncie Central dressing room to find every player in tears. We had been eliminated. Our season was over, and stone-cold dead were our hopes of becoming the first team to win the Indiana basketball championship five times. For three of the starters—all seniors—high school basketball had ended. There would be no next year.

One of these, a big center, had collapsed on the floor in a corner, heaving the racking sobs of pure heartbreak. The writer asked him, after a little, to take off his dirty, sweat-soaked uniform and get his shower.

"Don't want to take it off, Coach," he said. "I'll never get to put it on again."

We believe that this is the spirit that makes a team an athletic power. But we are running no basketball factory at Muncie Central and stress continually the fact that good school citizenship and good grades are far more to be desired than victories in any sport. Although we consider high school athletics reasonably serious business, we hope to keep our athletic program in good balance in relation to other school activities. We dont want basketball, or any sport, to "run" the school. Young men and women attend high school to obtain a share of the world's knowledge. Just as important, they are taught to live with one another and to become good parents, good citizens, good Americans. And we firmly believe that high school athletics, properly supervised, are of great importance in that training.

We have found that nearly all our athletes, having been exposed to team discipline, having learned to care for their bodies, and having experienced the soaring joy of victory and the bitter taste of defeat, become worthwhile members of their community. One became Mayor of Muncie in 1956. Another is chief of police. Others fill important positions in business, education, and industry. We are proud of them.

Daily practice schedule

Our daily practice schedule remains the same for the entire year. The only exception is the extension of time on some particular phase on which we need the work.

All of the boys are to be on the floor shooting by 3 P.M. each day. The only excuse we accept is for makeup schoolwork. Once the boy is on the floor, he remains until practice is over. No boy is allowed to leave the floor to get a drink. There are two exceptions: (1) injury and (2) to go to the rest room.

This practice schedule is in effect after the game season starts.

MONDAY

3:00 — 3:30	Shooting from all angles. Pivot men work on side baskets.
3:30 — 3:40	Warmup drills. Layup shots from all angles (shown in diagrams).
3:40 — 4:00	Correction of previous game's mistakes.
4:00 — 4:15	Setting up and explanation of next opponent's offense. Running of opponent's

offense, without our defense. Explanation of opponent's individuals and their duties in both offense and defense.

4:15 — 5:00   Assignment of defense to meet the opponent. Defense of the opponent's offense and out-of-bounds plays.

5:00 — 5:15   Running fundamentals to maintain condition.

5:15 — 5:30   Foul shooting. Five boys per basket. Each boy shoots two fouls; then group rotates.

TUESDAY

3:00 — 3:40   Same procedure as Monday.

3:40 — 4:00   Our offense without defense.

4:00 — 4:50   Scrimmage. Reserves use opponent's offense and defense. Mistakes are corrected during scrimmage. No jump balls are called. No fouls are called. No time-outs are called. We stop twice to let each boy shoot two fouls.

4:50 — 5:00   Special work, such as halfcourt press, overplaying, etc.

5:00 — 5:15   Foul shooting.

WEDNESDAY (Workday)

3:00 — 3:30   Shooting and layup drills (diagrammed). Some Wednesdays, nothing but fundamentals.

3:30 — 4:40   Scrimmage (same procedure as Tuesday's scrimmage).

4:40 — 5:00   Foul shooting.

THURSDAY

3:00 — 3:30	Shooting and layup drills.
3:30 — 3:45	Half-floor offense for timing.
3:45 — 4:00	Half-floor defense.
4:00 — 4:15	Practice out-of-bounds plays.
4:15 — 4:30	Practice defense against opponent's out-of-bounds plays.
4:30 — 4:50	Foul shooting.
4:50 — 5:00	Question period regarding opponents. If next game is away from home, the itinerary for travel is explained.

Every other Monday from 5:00 P.M. to 5:30 P.M. fast-break fundamentals are practiced. The "fast break" is stressed at all times during the weekly scrimmages.

Our conditioning comes from working hard all the time and from a lot of scrimmage. Use of the entire floor is stressed; seldom do we use half of the court. You cannot get your team in top condition by utilizing only half the floor.

This schedule is in effect at all times except during the Christmas holidays. During this time we review fundamentals—all phases—and scrimmage every day from 45 to 75 minutes. Christmas Day and Sundays are the only days practice is not held. Practice makes perfect.

Index

D

E

V

Z